THE
AMERICAN EMPIRE

THE WORLD IN FOCUS

THE AMERICAN EMPIRE

DEMOCRACY IN THE MIDDLE EAST

GLOBAL EXTREMISM
AND TERRORISM

**THE WORLD
IN FOCUS**

THE
AMERICAN
EMPIRE

JOHN C. DAVENPORT, SERIES EDITOR

CHELSEA HOUSE
PUBLISHERS

An imprint of Infobase Publishing

The American Empire

Copyright © 2007 by Infobase Publishing

Chelsea House
An imprint of Infobase Publishing
132 West 31st Street
New York, NY 10001

Library of Congress Cataloging-in-Publication Data

The American empire / [edited by] John C. Davenport.
    p. cm. — (The world in focus)
  Includes bibliographical references and index.
  ISBN-13: 978-0-7910-9195-1 (hardcover)
  ISBN-10: 0-7910-9195-3 (hardcover)
1. United States—Foreign relations—2001- 2. War on Terrorism, 2001-
3. Terrorism—Government policy—United States. 4. Imperialism. I. Davenport,
John, 1960- II. Title. III. Series.

  E895.A443 2007
  327.73—dc22

                                    2007003656

Chelsea House books are available at special discounts when purchased in bulk
quantities for businesses, associations, institutions, or sales promotions. Please
call our Special Sales Department in New York at (212) 967-8800 or (800) 322-
8755.

You can find Chelsea House on the World Wide Web at
http://www.chelseahouse.com.

Text design by James Scotto-Lavino
Cover design by Takeshi Takahashi

Printed in the United States of America

Bang FOF 10 9 8 7 6 5 4 3 2 1

This book is printed on acid-free paper.

All links and Web addresses were checked and verified to be correct at the time
of publication. Because of the dynamic nature of the Web, some addresses and
links may have changed since publication and may no longer be valid.

Contents Overview

———— ⧓ ————

Detailed Table of Contents

Introduction

⌒∞∞⌒

The swirl of twenty-first century current events can easily become overwhelming. With unprecedented speed, developments unfold, trends emerge, and crises arise. Every day, there seems to be more information demanding attention. Casual and expert observers alike carry a heavier burden of understanding, a weight made greater by the myriad interpretations of what takes place around the globe on a daily basis. Competing viewpoints crowd the marketplace of opinion; varying analyses of the latest issues vie for audiences and legitimacy. The resulting image of the modern world is thus blurred by abstraction and bias. People today, in short, have more difficulty than ever before in gaining a clear picture of what is going on around them. The challenge facing everyone, then, is to bring the world into focus.

This challenge is taken up in this series, a collection of three volumes that examine some of the most pressing and significant topics at the dawn of the new millennium. Each book plunges the reader into the disputes and debates that surround their subjects, assembling articles and excerpts from a variety of sources, including major books, the internet, and prestigious scholarly journals. Sifting through the various arguments and prescriptions offered by policy advocates, experts, and government agencies, *The World in Focus* examines three specific topic areas: Middle East democracy, American imperialism, and terrorism. The series explores each area in depth, then proceeds to lay out the many options for dealing with the problems associated with them. The arduous tasks of initiating democratic reform within Arab-Muslim society and politics, adapting to the reality of American hegemony, and combating extremism and terror are looked at in detail.

Throughout the volumes, multiple perspectives are reviewed, and a representative sample of contemporary thinking is offered. Authors expressing optimism concerning the chances for democratic change in the Middle East, for example, are coupled with those with more pessimistic outlooks. Supporters of the American assertion of imperial power are paired with its opponents. Writers who differ on the extent of the danger posed by global extremism, and the possible ways to counter it, are placed side by side. The reader will notice many voices in these three books, some more controversial than others. It is hoped that from this collection of analyses and interpretations, a deeper knowledge will be gained that might lead to better decision-making in the future.

DEMOCRACY IN THE MIDDLE EAST

There is perhaps no better place to start this process than the volatile Middle East. Plagued by a history of sectarian violence, repression, and colonialism, political evolution has been a bloody business for the Middle East in the past. Wars, assassination, and intrigue have often been the tools of choice among men and movements seeking to reshape the contours of power throughout a vast region that stretches from Africa to Asia. These struggles take place in an atmosphere charged further by the confluence of politics and Islam, a religion that shapes the lives of over one billion people.

Unsettled for centuries, the Middle East today serves as an arena for a monumental struggle between contesting political philosophies and systems. Traditional forms of autocracy and authoritarianism wrestle for dominance with newly imported strains of democracy. History favors the autocratic and authoritarian regimes that typify the Middle Eastern political landscape, but democracy is building momentum and gaining adherents, all the while being scrutinized for conformity to regional standards. Democracy is attractive to many people, but it must bear up under the strain of proving itself compatible with conservative social and religious norms. Some experts doubt democracy's chances for survival for these reasons; others are more hopeful. All of them, wary of making predictions, are guarded in their assessments.

Democracy in the Middle East presents their arguments and evaluations. It considers the prospects for democratic reform in a region notorious for tyranny, corruption, and inequity. The book's contributors weigh the odds that democratic institutions and political habits of thought can flourish there. Their essays and excerpts look at topics ranging from women's rights to the phenomenon of Muslim democracy. Each outlines and explains the powerful forces for both change and continuity in the Middle East and draws a conclusion as to whether or not democracy can flourish. The volume seeks to answer an important question: is there reason to hope that democracy might ever take root in such a troubled area?

THE AMERICAN EMPIRE

If so, the United States will almost certainly play a crucial role in its establishment. The United States has been and continues to be the most active agent for democratization in the Middle East. As a promoter of democracy, at least in theory, it is unsurpassed. But the American effort to export its political ideas and traditions is not limited to one region. The United States, in fact, is energetically working to reshape large parts of the world in its own image and create a universal political order that is liberal, democratic, secular, and built upon a solid foundation of consumer capitalism. The preferred tools for this job are cultural: movies, music, food, and fashion—but more muscular ones such as public diplomacy and even war are seen as equally valid and often more appropriate. The United States, put simply, has a vision of the world's future that is colored red, white, and blue.

Although viewed as benign or even benevolent by most Americans, many people in other countries wonder why the United States works so diligently to export its beliefs, customs, practices, and lifestyles. They question American motivations and intentions. Perhaps, it is thought, American actions signal a commitment to a better, freer future for everyone. On the other hand, they very well could indicate an insatiable imperial hunger for domination. Is the United States seeking to become a global hegemon? Or is it already a de facto imperial state, an empire in everything but name? What does all this mean for the rest of the humanity?

The American Empire studies these questions and tries to determine whether and to what extent the United States is an empire, what kind it is, and how enduring it will be. The articles and excerpts generally presume America's imperial status, then move on to consider the costs and benefits of such a position. They also seek to place the United States on the continuum of historical empires and come to a conclusion regarding whether the American empire might succeed where so many others have failed.

GLOBAL EXTREMISM AND TERRORISM

Regardless of America's imperial future, its current degree of influence worldwide often generates substantial fear and resentment. Coupled with its championing of Western-style democracy, America's assertiveness creates enemies. For many ethnic and religious groups, the United States' expressions of power evoke memories of European colonialism, exploitation, and oppression. Americans appear, to their eyes, to be just another band of arrogant foreigners bent on controlling the planet, its people, and its resources.

Not surprisingly, forces have emerged in resistance to American goals and objectives. Around the world, movements have sprung up in opposition to everything viewed as either a Western or specifically American import. Usually these movements employ peaceful means of protest. Sometimes, however, driven by local or regional impulses, they devolve into extremism and begin advocating more aggressive forms of reaction, up to and including violence. On occasion, movements transition from words to deeds; they transform themselves into terrorist cells and even transnational terrorist organizations. They adopt violence as both a strategy and tactic for advancing their anti-Western, anti-American agendas. Bombings, kidnappings, assassinations, and executions soon follow.

The third volume in *The World in Focus* surveys the dark and treacherous landscape of terrorism. *Global Extremism and Terrorism* seeks to define, describe, and illuminate the people who have chosen murder and mayhem as weapons in a war against belief systems and ways of life they view as evil. The book leads its readers into a violent netherworld where individuals and groups openly embrace destruction as a vehicle for change. The contributors look at who terrorists are and why they do the things they do. The often twisted motivations and justifications for destruction and the taking of innocent lives are dissected in search of some form of underlying logic. The chosen means of violence, ranging from piracy to suicide bombings, are explored and explained so that the audience can appreciate just how devastating the realization of terrorist plans can be. Lastly, *Global Extremism and Terrorism* weighs the options for counter-terrorist activity. How best to fight terrorism, and end its scourge, is a question for which tentative answers are offered. The world promises to become a far more dangerous place unless the agents of terror and their tools are better understood.

Taken together, the three books in this series sharpen the outlines of the modern world. They help lift the veil of confusion that too often obscures the popular views of current events, and reveal the inner structures of the issues that dominate today's headlines. A degree of blurriness will no doubt persist despite the best efforts of scholars and experts like those represented in *Democracy in the Middle East*, *The American Empire*, and *Global Extremism and Terrorism*. Nevertheless, each book does its part to clarify key global developments and, through close examination, bring them and the world into focus.

John C. Davenport
Series Editor

The Imperial Past

The word "empire," at first glance, seems deceptively easy to define: an independent state (say, a republic or kingdom) that exercises military, political, and economic control over other places outside of its borders. In truth, however, "empire" is a much more fluid term that changes depending upon when and where it is applied. The word adapts to the environment within which it operates, all the while describing the same basic set of characteristics in different combinations. Some places, therefore, appear to be empires and are not; others do not initially seem like empires, but really are. Complicating matters further is the fact that occasionally empires deny their very existence, even though their presence is obvious to everyone.

The United States is a prime example of a nation of such contradictions. It has been said that Americans "are a people on whom the mantle of empire sits uneasily . . . Yet, by any conventional standard . . . we are indeed an imperial power, possessed of an empire on which the sun truly never sets . . . Our impact reaches everywhere and affects everything it touches."* Historically, the United States, while issuing fervent denials of its imperial status, has behaved every bit like an empire. It has used armed force to conquer territory, acquire overseas possessions, establish protectorates, and gain economic dominance around the world, ruthlessly suppressing any indigenous resistance that arose in the process. Witness the North American Indian Wars (1811–1890), the Philippine Insurrection (1899–1902), and the Chinese Boxer Rebellion (1900). War and economic preeminence parallel one another in the American story, as they did in similar tales about the empires of Rome and Great Britain, among others.

Today, for instance, the U.S. military budget is 14 times the size of China's and 22 times that of Russia. The United States drives the global marketplace in terms of both luxury consumption and the development of high technology products. It also shapes the cultural desires of billions of people through its control of the various popular media. American English is the second language of 1 billion and the first of 400 million humans. "American" is spoken almost exclusively in international business, science, education, and entertainment. Even Rome's power, at its height, did not extend so far or run so deep.

Yet, for all its undeniably imperial qualities and accomplishments, the United States is a strange sort of empire. Its form and function differ in many ways from those that came before it. In fact, as Bruce Cumings argues, the term "empire" seems inadequate to describe fully and accurately America's status in the world today. He suggests

14

the use of the word "hegemon" instead. Hegemony, unlike traditional imperial rule, implies global power by consensus and leadership by acclaim. America, as a contemporary hegemon, is welcomed by the nations it dominates and thus has the unique opportunity to advance the security and welfare of the entire global community. Is the United States an empire? Perhaps, Cumings says, but an empire poised to do great service to humankind.

NOTES

*   Karl Meyer, *The Dust of Empire: The Race for Mastery in the Asian Heartland.* New York: Public Affairs, 2003, 21.

Is America an Imperial Power?
BRUCE CUMINGS

"That the United States would be hegemonic was inevitable from Bretton Woods onward. That it might also become an empire was not."

Who could have predicted that in the early years of the new millennium, the signature slogan of 1960s radicals, "American imperialism," would come roaring back to life? Several serious and substantial books have recently appeared in the United States with "empire" in the title, all trying to come to grips with the Brave New World created by George Bush and company.[1] Around the rest of the globe a debate rages over American power and "the echoes of empires past," in the words of *The New York Times'* Richard Bernstein. But is this a good way to think about the nature of contemporary American power in the world?

Empire is clearly a useful concept for understanding the history of the successive bureaucratic dynasties that ruled China until 1911, or the prewar capitalist empires such as those of Great Britain, France, and Japan, which rested on exclusively held territories known as colonies. It is not a useful concept, however, if we mean it, without any redefinition, to denote the United States and its current position in the world. To do so instantly runs afoul of the classic understanding of imperialism as some form of direct or monopoly control of another nation or of regions of the world economy (such as sterling blocs and franc blocs). No one argues that the United States possesses monopoly controls in the world economy or runs a set of territorial possessions lacking any attribute of national sovereignty. Empire might be redefined with various "post-" or "ultra" or "neo-" tags, but these also beg the question. If imperialism means direct or monopoly control and neo-imperialism does not, perhaps we need a different term. We certainly need an explication of the differences between classical and contemporary imperialism.

Michael Hardt and Antonio Negri dropped the term "imperialism" in their recent influential book *Empire*. They analyze current configurations of power in terms of "globalization," the phenomenon whose territorial realm knows no limit and whose mechanisms are driven by the International Monetary Fund (IMF), the World Bank, the World Trade Organization (WTO), the United Nations, multinational corporations, and a multitude of NGOs dedicated to causes ranging from humanitarian intervention to the nonproliferation of weapons of mass destruction. All share a common agenda: to set the rules for a new globalized world. The United States plays a critical and often determining role in this rule-setting—China's WTO application had to wait 15 years for Washington to approve it—but America is not the sole seat of this empire.

A broad-brush definition that would equate empire with globalization fails because it accumulates everybody, everything, and every organization that traces its beginnings to post–World War II arrangements, such as the Bretton Woods conference of 1944. Therefore, we cannot determine what is in and what is out of this empire. (Did the Chinese become part of it when the United States allowed them to join the WTO?) Globalization is nothing new, except to 20-something protesters around the world. In fact, it represents the outcome and ultimate fulfillment of American planning going back six decades.

ACHESON'S CREATION

In the immediate aftermath of Hitler's invasion of Poland in 1939, Dean Acheson first imagined the rules that would govern the postwar world. "Our vital interests do not permit us to be indifferent to the outcome" of the wars raging in Europe and Asia, the future secretary of state said in a speech at Yale. Nor could Americans remain isolated from such events— unless they wished a kind of eternal "internment on this continent." (Only an Atlanticist would liken North America to a concentration camp.) Acheson located the causes of the war and the global depression that preceded it in "the failure of some mechanisms of the Nineteenth Century world economy" that had led to "this break-up of the world into exclusive areas for armed exploitation administered along oriental lines." In its time, he said, "the economic and political system of the Nineteenth Century . . . produced an amazing increase in the production of wealth," but for many years it had been in an "obvious process of decline."

Reconstructing the foundations of peace and prosperity would require new mechanisms, Acheson asserted: new ways to make capital available for industrial production, the rapid removal of tariffs, "a broader market for goods made under decent standards," "a stable international monetary system," and the elimination of "exclusive or preferential trade arrangements." Acheson emphasized the world economy, but in good realpolitik fashion he also called for the immediate creation of a "navy and air force adequate to secure us in both oceans simultaneously and with striking power sufficient to reach to the other side of each of them."

This lawyer and statesman later had the opportunity to implement these ideas, first at Bretton Woods, then with the Marshall Plan and the Truman Doctrine in 1947, and finally, in 1950, with NSC-68, the executive order implementing the policy of "containing" communism. Acheson is the person who comes closest to being the singular architect of American strategy from 1944 to 1953—and he knew it (*Present at the Creation* was his memoir of the period). The captains of the American Century like Acheson were those who thought in "both/and" terms: Europe and Asia, the open door and partnership with imperial Britain, a world economy with no ultimate limit. As he later put it in reflecting back on his Yale speech, he had really sought at the time to "begin work on a new postwar world system."

The makers of the postwar order—Roosevelt, Stimson, Acheson, McCloy, Kennan, Lovett—were theorists (even if of a practical bent). They had ideas, and ideas have consequences. They were all liberal modern-ists, of course, but Acheson had a full appreciation of the theory of world economy while other architects of the postwar world, such as George Kennan, had almost none. British hegemony gave Acheson his model for how to run the world, conceived along the lines of Great Britain's role after 1815—not as an imperial colonizer, but as the power of last resort for keeping the world, and particularly the world economy, from spinning out of control. The name for American leadership in this sense was *hegemony*.

This term best captures the U.S. role in the world, understood as a consensual leadership in which the United States ranks first among equals, and where the ultimate goal is the growth and flourishing of a unified world economy. For four decades, however, American leaders achieved only a second-best world. The Soviet Union and the militarized and exclusively held empire that it created in postwar Eastern Europe were self-sufficient and well defended; the Soviet leaders could say *nyet* any time they wanted, and they did so all the time in the 1940s and 1950s. That reality essentially created the two-bloc, polarized cold war world from 1947 to 1991.

But the world also experienced a completely unanticipated history in the violent period of decolonization that lasted for three decades, until the Portuguese empire finally collapsed in 1975. The world witnessed bloody and disastrous wars in Korea and Vietnam, the ongoing reorientation of revolutionary China, and the ultimate collapse of the Soviet empire and Soviet Union—all experiences that would have flabbergasted a statesman seeking to chart the postwar order in 1945. Never could the Achesons and Stimsons have imagined the fierce energy of aroused colonial peoples in the 1940s, for whom classical imperialism and a recent feudal past were hated realities and the promises of liberal modernism, an utter chimera. Nor could the theory of totalitarianism that long ruled the minds of American planners conceive of the possibility that courageous people in myriad civil-society groups (beginning with Poland's Solidarity) would bring down Eastern European communism from within.

THE HEGEMON COMETH

The internationalist presuppositions molded into the bones of Acheson, Henry Stimson, Robert Lovett, and many others by the experience of the 1930s explain how our world order came into being. Kennan, the anonymous "Mr. X" author of an influential *Foreign Affairs* article that proposed containment of communism, is often considered the behind-the-scenes architect of the postwar global order. But Acheson was the true "Mr. X" of his time—and of ours. The globalized world materialized in its full glory after the end of the cold war, and was the anticipated fulfillment, if by a tortuous path, of the plans, hopes, and dreams of American and Western internationalists. They learned the searing lessons of the Great Depression and the world war that it spawned. They took guidance from an imperial British model of hegemonic leadership—minus the colonies—to become the power of last resort. Like England but in a much more egalitarian manner, the United States also filled out its national and material interests with the classic ideas of liberalism: liberty, democracy, freedom of speech, civil rights, civil society. Honored in the breach by the racially segregated America of the first two decades after World War II, these ideas nonetheless had revolutionary implications for much of the rest of the world.

Immanuel Wallerstein, drawing on the brilliant work of Karl Polanyi in his book, *The Great Transformation*, aptly defined hegemony as the simultaneous and temporary "productive, commercial and financial pre-eminence of one core [or advanced-industrial] power over other core powers." The critical element here is "productive advantage," which conditions the other two (commerce and finance). This conception assumes that the world market constitutes the primary mechanism and arena of hegemony—even if the term may also encompass empire, colonies, neocolonialism, and what is sometimes called informal empire. Military advantage, conventionally considered the essence of hegemony by realists such as John Mearsheimer, merely locks in hegemony after the fact.

Notably, too, the theory includes two senses of "temporary": an abnormal first phase of enormous competitive advantage against all others, which lasts only briefly, and the normal long phase of "temporary" hegemony in which a core state is primus inter pares. In America's case, the first temporary phase lasted from 1941 to 1971, driven by the vast economic and military power of the United States and the wartime destruction of the other industrial economies. By the time Richard Nixon became president, other economies had recovered, prompting in 1971 his announcement of a "New Economic Policy" directed against allied competitors. The United States accounted for half of all industrial production in 1945, and approximately 25 percent by Nixon's presidency. That is about where the United States is today, as well. In this crucial sense America has never been in decline, in spite of much 1980s commentary to the contrary. It remains in the middle age of hegemony—the second or long temporary phase—with many more decades left of relative predominance among the industrial powers.

The realm of this hegemonic "grand area" is bounded by the reach of the world market. As Polanyi emphasized, "market" means "world market": the market continuously expands, carrying before it settled societies, national boundaries, even the formerly impervious structures of the communist bloc. Or as Marx put it in "The Communist Manifesto," the world market "knocks down all Chinese walls." The limit on the market is society: human collectivities that strive ceaselessly to subordinate the rational imperatives and the cruel up-and-down cycles of the market to human control. Society often acts through the state, which is the gatekeeper between domestic society and the backwash of the world market. Thus the fundamental global dynamic is production for profit in a world market, limited and constrained by human collectivities.

THE LIBERAL MOMENT

For most of the postwar era, Republican centrists like John Foster Dulles, Henry Kissinger, and George Herbert Walker Bush agreed with cold war liberals in the Democratic Party on all of this, and just about everything else beyond the water's edge. A seamless consensus prevailed inside the Washington Beltway on containment, internationalism, the NATO and U.S.-Japan alliances, and the iron necessity to consult with American allies at the UN, IMF, or World Bank. Sometimes the result was unilateralism disguised as multilateralism (Korea, Vietnam). But everyone bespoke the internationalist mantras, and everyone knew that a consensual partnership, with the United States as first among (would-be) equals, offered the only lasting, sustainable hegemony.

The Clinton administration appeared to understand this American role better than any administration since the Truman and Roosevelt presidencies. The Clinton years incorporated an active foreign economic policy under the leadership of Treasury Secretary Robert Rubin, a seemingly omniscient central bank under Alan Greenspan, and a president who consulted every ally and friend to the point of (their) exhaustion in his search for multilateral consent and first-among-equals leadership—a charismatic figure received like a rock star in places as diverse as New Delhi, Beijing, Hanoi, Berlin, and the editorial offices of *The New Yorker* (where editor Tina Brown swooned over him). This leadership combined to achieve the full measure of what the 1940s founding fathers had imagined for the American role in the world, before the cold war dashed their hopes.

The members of the Clinton administration also—and they would say predictably—presided over the longest economic boom in postwar American history; involving great leaps forward in productivity from 1995 to 2000 that defied the assumptions of nearly all economists (and kept Greenspan scratching his head as to whether some kind of technological revolution was upsetting his conventional expectations). The new millennium thus appeared to catch the high tide of American hegemony. We all know Clinton's flaws, including those of his diplomacy and warfare, but in 2003 his leadership shines like a beacon—as if the Enlightenment were unaccountably followed by the Dark Ages.

ARCHIPELAGO OF EMPIRE

Is there nonetheless in some sense an "American empire?" We can begin again with the question of territorial control: What are the empire's boundaries? How do we rule one nation or area of the world in, and another out? Simply to pose this question is again to denote the differences between classical empires and the post-1945 American realm of action in the world. Empires, whether of the traditional or capitalist type, encompass territory. If the United States has run an empire since 1900 or so, it has been a nonterritorial empire. Until the recent past, the only way in which the term "empire" applied to America was in the multitude of military bases that it maintains around the world. In the aftermath of the wars in Afghanistan and Iraq, the United States has expanded this militarized structure to its farthest extent in history.

William Appleman Williams began the 1960s discourse on American empire with his classic 1959 book that influenced a generation of young people, *The Tragedy of American Diplomacy*. The United States had one or two colonies; like the Philippines. But what it really had since the 1890s, he thought, was an "open-door empire," merging the world economy with chunks of territorial control around the world, places where the United States dispatched the Marines (most of which were found in Central America). Is this America's empire? Perhaps, but in Joseph Schumpeter's sense and not Williams'. Schumpeter saw empire as an atavism similar to the later Roman empire—redoubling its expansive efforts after losing sight of its goals. He also saw imperialism as a policy choice that, once implemented, created in its wake a perpetual-motion machine dedicated to the service of empire. Forces called into being for one purpose remain long after they have lost sight of the purpose. This offers a way to think about the U.S. military-industrial complex and its contemporary role in policing a world grown far beyond the old boundaries of American power.

That the United States would be hegemonic was inevitable from Bretton Woods onward. That it might also become an empire was not. The project of hegemony offered a means to achieve the revival and flourishing of the world economy. The project of containment provided a way to draw lines in the sand against the communist adversary as well as a way to constrain capitalist allies (mainly Germany and Japan) by keeping military bases on their territory. In the wake of the end of the cold war and the Soviet Union's collapse, the hegemonic project continued. But so did the allied containment project, even though it lost sight of any formidable adversary. Punishing Saddam Hussein; isolating Cuba, obliterating potential nuclear "power" North Korea: these are small potatoes compared to the good old days of the cold war.

But the Pentagon, if not the White House, does run an empire. How might we specify its territory? It is in the first instance an archipelago of military bases—or what one U.S. general recently called "lily pads" around the world, useful for projecting American power. it was this vast and enduring complex that the collapse of the Soviet Union seemed to render obsolete. Yet Johnny never came marching home. When you think about it, Johnny never has since 1945. Win (World War II), lose (Vietnam) or draw (Korea), American troops never come home; 78,000 remain in Germany, nearly 100,000 in Japan and Korea. (Defeat did of course evict troops from Indochina, but not from the region.)

Now President George W. Bush has sponsored a massive outward thrust in this basing system, into Central and South Asia, Indonesia and the Philippines, and nearly every country in the Middle East willing to host troops. The military likes its foreign bases but does not deserve blame for the most recent expansion that has come in the wake of 9-11. Indeed, many at the heart of the matter resist this new crusade: Brigadier General Jared Kennish, who commanded troops in Kyrgyzstan, lamented: "Here I am in a nation I had never heard of, couldn't pronounce and couldn't find on a map six months ago...." Vice Admiral Lyle Bien told the same reporter, "We're developing a force that makes it almost too easy to intervene. I am concerned about America pounding herself out."[2]

Other parts of this military territory are harder to specify. Panama and the Philippines were "in" for a long time, whether by virtue of their many American military bases, or the ease and frequency with which the Marines came ashore (the three-year war to subdue Philippine insurgents in the early 1900s, many expeditions into Panama since the turn of the past century). But today the Panama command is gone, and so are Subic Bay and Clark Air Force base in the Philippines. Does that make Panama and the Philippines independent? Perhaps not, but it puts them outside the territorial realm of the "lily pad" archipelago. The second— and third—largest economies in the world, Japan and Germany, now America's primary economic competitors, remain part of the archipelago with American bases dotting their homeland. A country like Brazil or Poland falls out of this empire, but within the realm of hegemony. Both suffered severe foreign debt burdens in the 1980s, as does Brazil today, both eventually succumbed to the zealous ministrations of the IMF, and both remain firmly ensconced in the developing world.

"Empire" in this light is the relative and contingent, historically bound term; "hegemony," the name of the realm. The liberal world system did not necessarily need an American empire of military installations. Their spread resulted from the struggle with the anti-system and, as Roosevelt imagined in the 1940s, it did not have to happen that way. (Socialist regimes could have been accommodated within the hegemonic realm.) The world system did need a hegemon, however, which was the singular testimony of a singular decade: the 1930s. What England no longer could do the United States was not ready to do; the results were depression and war and the collapse of the old order.

UNILATERAL IMPERIALISM

World War II began for Americans in the Pacific, and it remained the main theater of American warfare until the invasion of Europe in 1944.

The United States was preeminent in the defeat of Japan, and proceeded to organize a unilateral occupation of Japan and a general reorganization of postwar East Asian international relations. After the Korean War, the United States maintained a permanent peacetime defense budget of between $300 billion and $500 billion in current dollars. At the same time the American military "locked in" its war gains from the defeat of Japan and the defense of South Korea and Taiwan with a series of military bases that (with the exception of Taiwan) still form the basis of American coercive power in Northeast Asia.

Since 1945 the United States has operated differently in East Asia compared with Europe, with an emphasis on unilateralism, bilateral rather than multilateral diplomacy, and the efficacy of military force. Likewise, the Republican Party has long embraced both tendencies: the free-trade multilateralism and Atlanticism of the Eastern wing, but also the expansionist, unilateralist outlook of Western Republicans, symbolized by the "Asia firsters" of the 1950s. The former was hegemonic on the British model, taking the world economy as its main arena of action. The latter was imperialist, beholden to the myths and realities of the frontier, the cowboy and the cavalry, and supporting unilateral expansion to the West, the subjugation of the Philippines, and eventually China (always, to these foreign affairs naifs, the "China" of their imagination). The reigning hero of this tendency was General Douglas MacArthur, a classic man on horseback, brutalizer of the Bonus Marchers, suzerain of the Philippines, conqueror of Japan who became its benign emperor for six years, only to suffer defeat at the hands of a Sino-Korean peasant army in 1950.

The Bush family history reflects a microcosm of ways to bring the party's Eastern and Western wings together. The father, George H.W., exemplifies a thoroughly Eastern Republican—born in Greenwich, Connecticut, combining internationalist foreign policy with great wealth and aristocratic privilege. His Texas credentials, honed since he moved there in the 1950s, never fooled anyone: he was as persuasive at a tent revival as Dick Cheney at a labor rally. The elder Bush served in government as a charter member of the internationalist consensus. George W., on the other hand, went Texan with a vengeance. He is the first president fully to embody the Republican right's foreign policy views on a host of issues: arms control, the environment, the United Nations, post-Soviet Russia, China, North Korea, Iraq, and the presumed failings of America's traditional European allies. His preemptive doctrine post 9-11 embodies phrases and nuances that had been the stock in trade of right-wing pundits such as William Kristol and Charles Krauthammer, who have long called for a new American imperialism. And in its implementation the Bush doctrine has become frankly imperialist, with the old archipelago of relatively quiescent military bases expanded into the equivalent of distant Roman legions.

THE LIMITS OF POWER

Any administration would have responded forcefully to the attacks of September 11, but Bush and his allies have vastly distended the Pentagon budget (from $265 billion In 2000 to $400 billion in 2003), added another zone of military containment (Central Asia), created an American West Bank the size of California in Iraq, and poured yet more billions into "Homeland Defense" while showing a callous disregard for civil liberties, the rights of the accused, and the views of America's traditional allies. Bush always begins his account of "the war on terrorism" with September 11, as if that watershed event convinced him to give up on the tested doctrine of containment and deterrence and to move instead to a new strategy of preemptive attack. The 9-11 attacks did indeed come from an implacable and diabolical enemy: nothing will deter it, and it passionately loves suicide. Containment would not scam Osama bin Laden even if he could be found. But the United States can do little about that threat, the past year of the "war on terrorism" notwithstanding.

In March 2003 the strategy of preemption quickly gave way to a preventive war against Iraq in an attempt to stop Saddam from possessing weapons of mass destruction (weapons that have yet to be found). So far the war in Iraq has not had the worst consequences for regional security that many critics worried about, even if the occupation has turned into an unholy nightmare. But a restive world may present an unavoidable crisis—most likely in North Korea—where containment and deterrence abruptly give way to preemption and disaster.

In September 2002 George Kennan, then 98, gave a little-noticed interview to *The Hill*, just after the National Security Council released Bush's new doctrine. Here was "a great mistake in principle," Kennan said. Anyone who has studied history "knows that you might start a war with certain things in your mind," but you end up fighting for things "never thought of before." Launching a second war with Iraq "bears no relation to the first war against terrorism," he remarked. Moreover a decision for war "should really rest with Congress" (but not with congressional Democrats, who have been "shameful and shabby" not to mention "timid," in their reaction to Bush's war plans). Here was distilled wisdom, drawn from a lifetime of service to the country's diplomacy. At some point, astute judgment like this about the inherent limits of American power will again become obvious to the people, as it did in

Vietnam a generation ago, and America's leaders will return to their only hope: leading with allies; forming coalitions with them acting as first among equals.

NOTES

1. Among several, see Andrew J. Bacinevich, *American Empire: The Reality and Consequences of US Diplomacy* (Cambridge: Harvard University Press, 2003); Niall Ferguson, *Empire: The Rise and Demise of the British World Order and the Lessons of Global Power* (New York: Basic Books, 2003); Michael Hardt and Antonio Negri, *Empire* (Cambridge: Harvard University Press, 2002). Harvard professor Michael Ignatieff has published two recent articles on U.S. imperialism in *The New York Times Magazine*. Even presidential candidates are getting into the act: see General Wesley Clark, *Winning Modern Wars: Iraq, Terrorism and the American Empire* (New York: Public Affairs, 2003).

2. Greg Jaffe, "Pentagon Prepares to Scatter Soldiers in Remote Corners," *The Wall Street Journal* (May 27, 2003), pp. A1, A6. However, the deputy commander of the Manas Air Field near Kyrgyz, Col. James Forrest, told Jaffe that "this place is so deep into Central Asia you'd hate to lose it," a good indication that this former Soviet base is not likely to be "lost" to the Pentagon anytime soon.

It is easy to quarrel with the use of the term "empire" to describe the United States. The nation neither looks nor acts like the great empires of days past, making it a bit of a stretch to place modern America in the company of ancient Persia, imperial Rome, and nineteenth-century Great Britain. Even if the name and historical association fit uncomfortably, imperial objectives have often stood at the center of American relations with the rest of the world. Such has been the case since the original 13 colonies gained their independence—ironically, from an empire—in 1783. The country's founders, for their part, often acknowledged an imperial impulse behind American aspirations for the future and rarely shied away from the word "empire." In fact, unlike their modern counterparts, they openly embraced it. Thomas Jefferson went so far as to advocate not just the concept, but also the functioning reality of empire. The American people, he wrote, were destined to rule over "an extensive empire . . . one of the greatest and most formidable that ever was in the world."*

Jefferson, and others like him, foresaw an American empire built on a solid foundation of democracy and liberal Enlightenment values, such as limited government, individual freedom, popular rule, and equality of opportunity. Uniquely blessed with these things by God, they believed, America was tasked to export those blessings abroad. It was thought that the United States could create and manage what Max Boot, in the following essay, calls a "liberal empire," encompassing first North America and then the world, bestowing freedom and justice on humanity.

Boot claims that Jefferson's "empire of liberty" is on the verge of becoming a reality, and a beneficial one at that. The United States, he writes, "aims to instill democracy in lands that have known tyranny," just as the third American president had instructed. If this effort is successful, the world as a whole can expect a better future, one characterized by progress, order, and respect for human rights. The legacy of such a liberal imperial quest, in the author's opinion, is bound to be a positive one.

NOTES

*   Robert W. Tucker and David C. Hendrickson, *Empire of Liberty: The Statecraft of Thomas Jefferson.* New York: Oxford University Press, 1990, ix.

Neither New nor Nefarious:
The Liberal Empire Strikes Back
MAX BOOT

President George W. Bush came to office condemning the "nation building" undertaken by his predecessor in Haiti, Bosnia, and Kosovo. Yet circumstances beyond his control have forced the president to revise his stance. Since September 11, 2001, the United States has launched ambitious nation-building efforts in Afghanistan and Iraq. Despite being hobbled by a lack of resources and long-term planning, the U.S. forces trying to remake these two countries have undoubtedly improved life for their people. Whether America will succeed in planting the seeds of democracy remains a question whose answer will not be known for years to come, but the intent—to leave these places better off—should be evident to everyone.

The historical record provides some perspective on the challenges facing the United States in its latest bout of what might be called "liberal imperialism." For obvious reasons, government officials shy away from the term. When asked on April 28, 2003, on the Arabic satellite television network al Jazeera whether the United States was "empire building," Secretary of Defense Donald Rumsfeld reacted as if he had been asked whether he wears women's underwear. "We don't seek empires," he replied huffily. "We're not imperialistic. We never have been."

That is a fine answer for public consumption. The problem is that it is not true. The United States has been an empire since at least 1803, when Thomas Jefferson purchased the Louisiana Territory. Throughout the nineteenth century, what Jefferson called the "empire of liberty" expanded across the continent. When U.S. power stretched from "sea to shining sea," the American empire moved abroad, acquiring colonies ranging from Puerto Rico and the Philippines to Hawaii and Alaska.

While the formal empire mostly disappeared after World War II, the United States set out on another bout of imperialism in Germany and Japan. It was called "occupation" rather than imperialism, but when Americans are running foreign governments, this is a distinction without a difference. Likewise, recent "nation-building" experiments in Somalia, Haiti, Bosnia, Kosovo, Afghanistan, and Iraq amount to imperialism under another name. Not the old-fashioned imperialism bent on looting nations of their natural resources—if that were the motivation it is hard to see why America would intervene in some of the poorest countries on the planet, such as Afghanistan and Haiti. Iraq, of course, does have vast oil reserves, but the cost of the military occupation (which has already soared over $100 billion) will far exceed any possible economic benefits the United States will derive from guaranteeing uninterrupted access to the country's oil supply.

BACK TO NATION BUILDING

Compared with the grasping old imperialism of the past, America's "liberal imperialism" pursues far different, and more ambitious, goals. It aims to instill democracy in lands that have known tyranny, in the hope that doing so will short-circuit terrorism, military aggression, and weapons proliferation. This is an ambitious undertaking, the most successful examples of which are post–World War II Germany, Italy and Japan. In those cases, the U.S. Army helped transform militaristic dictatorships into pillars of liberal democracy—one of the most significant developments of the twentieth century.

Critics of nation building question the relevance of these examples to today's world. Germany, Italy, and Japan were advanced industrialized nations that had some experience with the rule of law and democratic institutions. And besides, the United States made a very large, very long-term commitment to those countries, a commitment justified by their importance to the world, but one that America has not so far made in any of the places where it has intervened in the past decade. Under the Marshall Plan, the United States poured $79 billion in current dollars into Europe between 1948 and 1952. By contrast, the United States has committed far smaller amounts in economic assistance to Afghanistan and Iraq.

Fair enough. Let us leave Germany, Italy, and Japan aside, and look at the U.S. peacekeeping record in what is now known as the third world. Between the Spanish-American War and the Great Depression, the United States embarked on an ambitious attempt at "progressive" imperialism in the Caribbean, Central America, and the Pacific. Successive administrations, from McKinley's to Wilson's, were emboldened to act by a variety of concerns. These included strategic reasons (keeping foreign powers out of areas deemed vital to U.S. interests, such as the Panama Canal Zone) and economic reasons (expanding opportunities for American businesses in promising markets, such as China). Above all, there was the weight of "The White Man's Burden," the title of a famous poem written in 1899 by Rudyard Kipling in an attempt to persuade Washington to annex the Philippine Islands.

The United States did annex the Philippines. It also occupied a number of territories that, under various legal guises, remain part of the United States to this day: Samoa, Guam, Hawaii, Puerto Rico, and the Virgin Islands. America occupied a number of other places temporarily in addition to the Philippines: the Panama Canal Zone, Haiti, the Dominican Republic, Nicaragua, and the Mexican city of Veracruz. The duration of occupation ranged from seven months (in Veracruz) to almost a century (in the Canal Zone). In the process, the United States produced a set of colonial administrators and soldiers who would not have been out of place on a veranda in New Delhi or Nairobi. Men like Leonard Wood, the dashing former Army surgeon and Rough Rider, who went on to administer Cuba and the Philippines; Charles Magoon, a stolid Nebraska lawyer who ran the Panama Canal Zone and then Cuba during the second U.S. occupation (1906–1909); and Smedley Butler, the "Fighting Quaker," a marine who won two Congressional Medals of Honor in a career that took him from Nicaragua to China.

These were tough, colorful, resourceful operators who used methods not found in any training manual. The story of the Haitian-U.S. Treaty of 1915, which gave a legal gloss to an American occupation that would last 19 years, captures the period. For years marines told one another that when Major Butler was sent to the presidential palace to obtain the signature of President Philippe Sudre Dartiguenave, the president, not wanting to sign, hid in his bathroom. Butler simply commandeered a ladder and climbed up through the bathroom window to present the treaty and a pen to the startled Dartiguenave. "Sign here," the major commanded, and the president did. Whether or not this "gorgeous legend" (as one marine called it) is actually true, it gives an accurate flavor of how U.S. rule was consolidated.

PATTERNS OF OCCUPATION

Most of these occupations followed a pattern. The United States was usually drawn in by political unrest and a threat to its foreign financial interests; Washington often feared that if it did not act, some other power would. The United States would then occupy the capital, and its armed forces, usually a handful of marines, would fan out over the countryside to establish order. Often some guerrilla resistance materialized, but it was usually put down quickly by a small number of American troops, who had more sophisticated weaponry and (even more important) better training. In Haiti in 1915, 2,000 marines pacified a country of 2 million people, at a cost of only 3 dead Americans. America waged its longest and most arduous colonial campaign in the

Philippines. It took 70,000 soldiers four years, suffering more than 4,000 casualties, to consolidate U.S. control over the islands.

Once its rule was firmly established, the United States would set up a constabulary, a quasi-military police force led by Americans and made up of local enlisted men. Then the Americans would work with local officials to administer a variety of public services, from vaccinations and schools to tax collection. American officials, though often resented, usually proved more efficient and less venal than their native predecessors.

A priority was improving public health, partly out of altruism and partly to keep U.S. troops themselves healthy in a tropical clime. Cuba set the pattern. There Walter Reed, an Army doctor, proved that yellow fever was spread by a particular variety of mosquito. A mosquito-eradication campaign undertaken at gunpoint drastically reduced the incidence of malaria and yellow fever, which had been ravaging the island for centuries. In Veracruz in 1914, Army General Frederick Funston cleaned up the water supply, improved sewage, and even imported 2,500 garbage cans from the United States. The death rate among city residents plummeted. U.S. forces are undertaking similar public health campaigns in Iraq today.

American imperialists usually moved much more quickly than their European counterparts to transfer power to democratically elected local rulers—as they are attempting to do in Iraq initially by setting up a governing council of Iraqis. In 1907, under U.S. rule, the Philippines became the first Asian state to establish a national legislature. In 1935 the archipelago became a domestically autonomous commonwealth headed by President Manuel Quezon, a former insurrectionist who once complained of the difficulty of fostering nationalism under this particular colonial regime: "Damn the Americans! Why don't they tyrannize us more?" (Total independence came in 1946, after Filipinos had fought side by side with GIs against the Japanese.)

In many of the countries that the United States occupied, holding fair elections became a top priority because once a democratically elected government was installed, the Americans felt they could withdraw. In 1925 the Coolidge administration refused to recognize the results of a stolen election in Nicaragua and the following year sent in the marines, even though the strongman who had stuffed the ballot boxes, General Emiliano Chamorro Vargas, was ardently pro-American. The United States went on to administer two elections in Nicaragua, in 1928 and 1932, that even the losers acknowledged were the fairest in the country's history. "The interventions by U.S. Marines in Haiti, Nicaragua, the Dominican Republic and elsewhere in those years," writes the Harvard political scientist Samuel Huntington, "often bore striking resemblances to the interventions by Federal marshals in the conduct of elections in the American South in the 1960s: registering voters, protecting against electoral violence, ensuring a free vote and an honest count."

That is certainly not the popular impression. The interventions in Central America and the Caribbean have become infamous as "gunboat diplomacy" and "banana wars" undertaken at the behest of powerful Wall Street interests. Smedley Butler helped solidify this myth when, after his retirement from the Marine Corps, he became an ardent isolationist and anti-imperialist. He spent the 1930s denouncing his own career, claiming he had been "a racketeer for capitalism" and a "high-class muscle man for Big Business."

In fact, in the early years of the twentieth century, the United States was least likely to intervene in those nations (such as Argentina and Costa Rica) where American investors held the biggest stakes. The longest occupations were undertaken in precisely those countries— Nicaragua, Haiti, the Dominican Republic—where the United States had the smallest economic stakes. Moreover, two of the most interventionist presidents in American history Theodore Roosevelt and Woodrow Wilson, were united in their contempt for what TR called "malefactors of great wealth." Wilson was probably the most imperialist president of all, and his interventions had a decidedly idealistic tinge. His goal, as he proclaimed at the start of his administration, was "to teach the South American republics to elect good men."

LEGACIES OF EMPIRE

How well did the United States achieve this aim? The record is mixed. Its greatest success (outside those territories that remain under the Stars and Stripes to this day) was in the Philippines—which, uncoincidentally, was also the site of one of its longest occupations. Among the institutions that Americans bequeathed to the Filipinos were public schools, a free press, an independent judiciary, a modern bureaucracy, democratic government, and separation of church and state. Unlike the Dutch in the East Indies, the British in Malaya, or the French in Indochina, the Americans left virtually no legacy of economic exploitation; Congress was so concerned about protecting the Filipinos that it barred large landholdings by American individuals or corporations. The U.S. legacy was also lasting: the Philippines have been for the most part free and democratic save for the period from 1972 to 1986, when Ferdinand Marcos ruled by fiat, which is more than most other Asian countries can say.

The U.S. legacy in the Caribbean and Central America was more fleeting. It is not true, as some critics later charged, that the United States deliberately installed dictators such as Duvalier, Batista, and Somoza. The governments left in power by American troops were usually democratic and decent. But they were also too weak to survive on their own. At one time the United States might have intervened to support democratically elected regimes. In the 1930s, however, President Franklin D. Roosevelt renounced the interventionist policies of his predecessors, including his cousin Theodore. Henceforth, FDR said, U.S. relations with Latin America would be governed by the "Good Neighbor" policy, which meant in essence that Washington would work with whoever came to power, no matter how.

The U.S. ambassador to Managua, Arthur Bill Lane, was shocked and upset when Anastasio Somoza, the commander of the Nicaraguan National Guard, murdered the former rebel leader Augusto Sandino and deposed the democratically elected president (who was also his uncle), Dr. Juan Bautista Sacasa. Lane wanted to intervene, as the United States might have in the past; but Roosevelt refused. Of Somoza, FDR famously (if perhaps apocryphally) said, "He may be a son of a bitch, but he's our son of a bitch." But make no mistake: Somoza did not attain power because of America's support; he attained power because of its indifference. The same might be said of François ("Papa Doc") Duvalier in Haiti, Rafael Trujillo in the Dominican Republic, and other dictators who took over after U.S. withdrawal.

Although its effects often wore off, U.S. rule looks pretty good by comparison with what came before and after in most countries. Haiti offers a particularly dramatic example. Before the U.S. occupation in 1915, seven presidents had been overthrown in seven years. After the last U.S. marines left in 1934, the country lapsed back into instability until, in 1957, the black nationalist Duvalier assumed power. He and "Baby Doc" (his son Jean Claude) ruled continuously until 1986, presiding over a reign of terror undertaken by their savage secret police, the Tontons Macoutes. After Baby Doc's overthrow it was back to chaos, leavened only by despotism. In 1994 the United States was driven to intervene once again to oust a military junta and restore to power President Jean Bertrand Aristide. But no matter who is in charge, the Haitian people continue to suffer horrifying levels of poverty, crime, disease, and violence; their country is the poorest in the Western Hemisphere, and one of the poorest on earth.

By contrast, the almost two decades of American occupation stand out as an oasis of prosperity and stability. While not exactly democratic (the United States ruled for a time through an appointed president), the American occupation was undertaken with minimal force. Haiti hosted fewer than 800 U.S. marines, and life was freer than at just about any time before or since. The Americans made no attempt to exploit Haiti economically; U.S. authorities actively discouraged large American companies from setting up shop for fear that they would take advantage of the people. The U.S. administrators ran the government fairly and efficiently, and by the time they left they could tick off a long list of achievements: 1,000 miles of roads and 210 bridges built, 9 major airfields, 1,250 miles of telephone lines, 82 miles of irrigation canals, 11 modern hospitals, 147 rural clinics, and on and on.

Unfortunately, most of the physical manifestations of the American empire—roads, hospitals, telephone systems—began to crumble not long after the marines pulled out. This should be no surprise; it has been the case whenever more technologically advanced imperialists have left a less sophisticated area, whether they were the Romans pulling out of Britain or the British out of India. The two most lasting legacies of American interventions in the Caribbean may be a resentment of the Yanquis, now perhaps fading, and a love of baseball, still passionately felt.

This does not mean, however, that occupation is entirely futile. U.S. troops can stop the killing, end the chaos, create a breathing space, and establish the rule of law. What the inhabitants do then is up to them. If America's aim is to recreate Ohio in Kosovo or Haiti, the occupiers are doomed to disappointment. But if the goals are more modest, U.S. rule can serve the interests of occupiers and occupied alike. Put another way, nation building is generally too ambitious a task, but state building is not, the apparatus of a functioning state can be developed much more quickly than a national consciousness.

HOW TO BUILD A STATE

Most successful examples of state building begin by imposing the rule of law—as the United States did in the Philippines, and Britain in India—which is a prerequisite for economic development and the eventual emergence of democracy. Merely holding an election and leaving will likely achieve little, as the United States learned in Haiti in 1994. For occupation to have a meaningful impact, it should be fairly lengthy; if Americans are intent on a quick "exit strategy;" they might as well stay home.

History teaches another important lesson: that occupation duty sometimes leads troops to commit what are today called human rights abuses. It is easy to exaggerate the extent of these excesses. Brian Linn's recent history, *The Philippine War, 1899–1902*, suggests that the conduct of American soldiers from 1899 to 1902 was not nearly as reprehensible as everyone from Mark Twain to New Left historians of the 1960s would have us believe.

But whenever a small number of occupation troops are placed in the midst of millions of potentially hostile foreigners, some unpleasant episodes are likely to occur. During the U.S. occupation of the Dominican Republic from 1916 to 1924, a marine captain named Charles F. Merkel became notorious as the Tiger of Seibo; he personally tortured one prisoner by slashing him with a knife, pouring salt and orange juice into the wounds, and then cutting off the man's ears. Merkel killed himself in jail after, rumor had it, a visit from two marine officers who left him a gun with a single bullet in it. When word of such abuses reached the United States, it caused a public uproar. In the 1920 election the Republican presidential candidate, Warren G. Harding, sought black votes by denouncing the "rape" of Hispaniola perpetrated by a Democratic administration. This kind of criticism is not so different from the questions raised today about U.S. treatment of Taliban or Iraqi prisoners.

American troops must take great care to avoid heinous conduct, not only for moral but also for practical reasons. If imperialists are provoked into too many grisly reprisals—as the French were in Algeria, or the Americans in Vietnam—support for their enterprise back home is likely to evaporate. And it is also much harder to win the "hearts and minds" of uncommitted civilians if you are routinely torturing or killing their relatives. Some mistaken shootings notwithstanding, this is a danger that U.S. troops have largely avoided in Afghanistan and Iraq.

It is inevitable that any nation bent on imperialism will encounter setbacks. The British army suffered major defeats with thousands of casualties in the first Anglo-Afghan War (1838–1842) and the Anglo-Zulu War (1879). This did not appreciably dampen Britain's determination to defend and extend its empire. If Americans cannot adopt a similarly tough-minded attitude, they have no business undertaking nation building. This is not to suggest that America should sacrifice thousands of young men for ephemeral goals, but that policymakers need to recognize that all military operations run certain risks, and the United States should not flee at the first casualty. More important, Washington should not design these operations (as it did with the occupation of Haiti in 1994) with the primary goal of producing no casualties. That is a recipe for ineffectuality.

THE IMPERIAL IMPERATIVE

Given the costs, moral and material, what is the case for undertaking imperialism at all? It is not so different today from 100 years ago. There is the economic argument: the United States can add areas such as Central Asia and the Balkans to the world free-trade system, within which America prospers. (These regions might seem like economic basket cases today, but so, a few decades ago, did Taiwan and South Korea. Both have prospered under U.S. military protection.) There is also the idealistic argument: the United States has a duty to save people from starvation, ethnic cleansing, and tyranny. This is a direct descendant of the "white man's burden," except today it is not limited to whites or to men but extends to everyone in the West. If these were the only reasons for America to undertake nation building, then it would be a hard sell, as indeed it was for large segments of the public in the 1990s. But since 9-11, another argument for imperialism has come to the fore: national security.

We can only wonder what might have happened if, after the Soviet Union was driven out in the early 1990s, the United States had helped build Afghanistan into a viable state. It might not have become the home of the Taliban and Al Qaeda, and the World Trade Center might still be standing.

This is only speculation, of course. But in the Balkans we can already see a payoff from nation building undertaken by the United States and its allies. The violence that claimed some 300,000 lives during the breakup of Yugoslavia is over. Kosovo, Macedonia, Croatia, Serbia, Slovenia, and Bosnia live in a state of uneasy peace under the eyes of Western troops. Aside from saving lives, there is another reason for the United States to take satisfaction in this outcome: Islamic extremists, who migrated to the Balkans in the early 1990s to help their fellow Muslims in Kosovo and Bosnia resist Serb oppression, have been denied a toehold in the region. NATO troops have been able to arrest and deport a number of terrorist suspects in Albania and Bosnia before they could blow up American installations. If U.S. troops had never intervened in the first place, it is likely that the Balkans would have turned into another Afghanistan, a refuge for terrorists, and this one located near the heart of Europe. Similar action may be necessary to drain other potential swamps that breed crime and violence. In Iraq, in particular, the United States has an opportunity to begin transforming an entire region—the Middle East—that has emerged as the greatest threat to American security since the demise of the Soviet Union.

Any call for a renewed campaign of nation building by Western states is likely to run into an obvious objection: Did imperialism not go out of style decades ago, when European administrators were chased out of one colony after another? True enough. Europeans found that the cost of ruling third world countries whose young men were fired up by nationalist doctrines was too high to pay. Then, too, in the wake of the Holocaust, the racist assumptions that had justified a small number of whites ruling over millions of non-white people lost their intellectual respectability. The British withdrew more or less gracefully from most of their empire, while the French fought to keep Vietnam and Algeria and suffered humiliating defeats. If the Europeans, with their long tradition of colonialism, have found the price of empire too high, what chance is there that Americans, whose country was born in a revolt against empire, will replace the colonial administrators of old?

Not much. The kind of imperial missions that the United States is likely to undertake today are very different. The Europeans fought to subjugate "natives"; Americans will fight to bring them democracy and the rule of law. (No one wants to put Iraq or Afghanistan permanently under the Stars and Stripes.) European rule was justified by racial prejudices; American interventions are justified by self-defense and human rights doctrines accepted (at least in principle) by all signatories to the Universal Declaration of Human Rights. European expeditions were unilateral; American missions are usually blessed with international approval; whether from the United Nations, NATO, or simply an ad hoc coalition. Even the U.S. intervention in Iraq this year, widely held to be "unilateral," enjoys far more international support (and hence legitimacy) than, say, the French role in Algeria in the 1950s.

This is not to suggest that American attempts at nation building are destined to be easy or painless. Dealing with local warlords is a difficult task that, if mishandled, can lead to disaster, as in Lebanon in 1983 or Somalia in 1993. Nor has pacifying Iraq proved as easy as some optimists expected. Many months after the fall of Saddam Hussein's government, guerrillas continue to attack U.S. troops and continue to inflict casualties. Still, it is important to note that these days the bulk of ordinary people are likely to support, at least in the beginning, an American peacekeeping presence in their country. From Kosovo to Afghanistan and even to most parts of Iraq (especially those areas dominated by Kurds and Shiites), GIs are seen as liberators, not oppressors. Many inhabitants of these war-torn lands want American troops to stay as long as possible. Unfortunately many policymakers in Washington, and many lawmakers on Capitol Hill, pine for an early "exit strategy" from places like Iraq and Afghanistan. The question is whether America will have the long-term staying power to leave a positive legacy from its recent experiments in nation building.

Reprinted with permission from *Current History* magazine (November 2003). © 2006 Current History, Inc.

Max Boot looks into the past and sees hope for the future, but most Americans rarely look backward into time. They are notorious for their ignorance of history. Americans as a people, in the words of writer Karl Meyer, "tend to dismiss anything that occurred even a year ago as ancient and irrelevant history."* Perhaps Sam Dillon of the *New York Times* said it best: "many Americans are, for all practical purposes, historically illiterate."** It is not surprising, then, that few Americans have a good understanding of their own imperial past. Schools, the media, and politicians rarely speak of U.S. history in an imperial context, preferring to use vague phrases such as the "American project" to describe the process of becoming globally dominant. American society, therefore, remains essentially blind to a key component of its developmental past.

This state of affairs could be shrugged off were it not for the fact of American preeminence. As the world's premier military superpower and economic colossus, the United States today has the ability to exercise its will at any point of its choosing. As was the case with the great empires of yesteryear, the application of such power is often a bloody matter, played out in wars large and small. Most of these are eventually forgotten, especially those battled out in obscure regions of the globe. The current war in Iraq may fall into this category, even if it momentarily occupies a central location in the American consciousness. The problem is that most people, unaware of their nation's imperial past, assume that Iraq is the first place to have felt the force of American might. For many in the general public, this is, with the possible exception of Vietnam, the one and only imperial "little war."

The author of the following article, John B. Judis, reminds his readers that Iraq is nothing new. The United States has flexed its muscles at other times in the names of progress, prosperity, and democracy. Judis points back toward America's early adventures in the Philippines (1898–1902) and Mexico (1916–1917), and recalls some of the first encounters between the American military and indigenous peoples. He asks his readers to educate themselves and to throw off the blinders that prevent a thorough appreciation of the centuries-old American imperial program.

NOTES

*   Karl Meyer, *The Dust of Empire: The Race for Mastery in the Asian Heartland.* New York: Public Affairs, 2003, xviii.

** Sam Dillon, "From Yale to Cosmetology School, Americans Brush up on History and Government," *New York Times*, September 9, 2005, A12.

Imperial Amnesia
JOHN B. JUDIS

The United States invaded a distant country to share the blessings of democracy. But after being welcomed as liberators, U.S. troops encountered a bloody insurrection. Sound familiar? Don't think Iraq—think the Philippines and Mexico decades ago. U.S. President George W. Bush and his advisors have embarked on a historic mission to change the world. Too bad they ignored the lessons of history.

On October 18, 2003, U.S. President George W. Bush landed in Manila as part of a six-nation Asian tour. The presidential airplane, Air Force One, was shepherded into Philippine airspace by F-15 fighter jets due to security concerns over a possible terrorist attack. Bush's speech to the Philippine Congress was delayed by what one reporter described as "undulating throngs of protestors that lined his motorcade route past shantytowns and rows of shacks." Outside the Philippine House of Representatives, several thousand more demonstrators greeted Bush, and several Philippine legislators staged a walkout during his 20-minute address.

In that speech, Bush credited the United States for transforming the Philippines into a democracy. "America is proud of its part in the great story of the Filipino people," said Bush. "Together our soldiers liberated the Philippines from colonial rule." He drew an analogy between the United States' attempt to create democracy in the Philippines and its effort to create a democratic Middle East through the invasion and occupation of Iraq. "Democracy always has skeptics," the president said. "Some say the culture of the Middle East will not sustain the institutions of democracy. The same doubts were once expressed about the culture of Asia. These doubts were proven wrong nearly six decades ago, when the Republic of the Philippines became the first democratic nation in Asia."

As many Philippine commentators remarked afterward, Bush's rendition of Philippine-American history bore little relation to fact. True, the U.S. Navy ousted Spain from the Philippines in the Spanish-American War of 1898. But instead of creating a Philippine democracy, the McKinley administration, its confidence inflated by victory in that "splendid little war," annexed the country and installed a colonial administrator. The United States then waged a brutal war against the same Philippine independence movement it encouraged to fight against Spain. The war dragged on for 14 years. Before it ended, about 120,000 U.S. troops were deployed, more than 4,000 were killed, and more than 200,000 Filipino civilians and soldiers were killed. Resentment lingered a century later during Bush's visit.

As for the Philippines' democracy, the United States can take little credit for what exists and some blame for what doesn't. The electoral machinery the United States designed in 1946 provided a democratic veneer beneath which a handful of families, allied to U.S. investors— and addicted to kickbacks—controlled the Philippine land, economy, and society. The tenuous system broke down in 1973 when Philippine politician Ferdinand Marcos had himself declared president for life. Marcos was finally overthrown in 1986, but even today Philippine democracy remains more dream than reality. Three months before Bush's visit, a group of soldiers staged a mutiny that raised fears of a military coup. With Islamic radicals and communists roaming the countryside, the Philippines is perhaps the least stable of Asian nations. If the analogy between the United States' "liberation" of the Philippines and of Iraq holds true, it will not be to the credit of the Bush administration, but to the skeptics who charged that the White House undertook the invasion of Baghdad with its eyes wide shut.

Politicians often rewrite history to their own purposes, but, as Bush's remarks suggested, there was more than passing significance to his revisionist account of the Spanish-American War. It reflected not just a distorted view of a critical episode in U.S. foreign policy but the rejection of important, negative lessons that Americans later drew from their brief experiment in creating an overseas empire. The United States' decision to invade and occupy Iraq wasn't, of course, a direct result of this misreading of the past. If Bush or Vice President Dick Cheney or Deputy Secretary of Defense Paul Wolfowitz (the administration's leading neoconservative) had remembered the brutal war the United States fought in the Philippines or similar misadventures in Mexico, or the blighted history of Western imperialism in the Middle East, they still might have invaded Iraq. But they also might have had second, third, or even fourth thoughts about what Bush, unconsciously echoing the imperialists of a century ago, called a "historic opportunity to change the world."

DIVINE INTERVENTIONISM

Prior to the annexation of the Philippines, the United States stood firmly against countries acquiring overseas colonies, just as American colonists once opposed Britain's attempt to rule them. But by taking over parts of the Spanish empire, the United States became the kind of imperial power it once denounced. It was now vying with Britain, France, Germany, Russia, and Japan for what future U.S. President Theodore Roosevelt called "the domination of the world."

Some Americans argued the country needed colonies to bolster its military power or to find markets for its capital. But proponents of imperialism, including Protestant missionaries, also viewed overseas expansion through the prism of the country's evangelical tradition. Through annexation, they insisted, the United States would transform other nations into communities that shared America's political and social values and also its religious beliefs. "Territory sometimes comes to us when we go to war in a holy cause," U.S. President William McKinley said of the Philippines in October 1900, "and whenever it does the banner of liberty will float over it and bring, I trust, the blessings and benefits to all people." This conviction was echoed by a prominent historian who would soon become president of Princeton University. In 1901, Woodrow Wilson wrote in defense of the annexation of the Philippines: "The East is to be opened and transformed, whether we will or no; the standards of the West are to be imposed upon it; nations and peoples which have stood still the centuries through are to be quickened and to be made part of the universal world of commerce and of ideas which has so steadily been a-making by the advance of European power from age to age."

The two presidents who discovered that the U.S. experiment with imperialism wasn't working were, ironically, Wilson and Theodore Roosevelt. Roosevelt had been an enthusiastic supporter of the U.S. takeover of the Spanish empire. "[I]f we do our duty aright in the Philippines," he declared in 1899, "we will add to that national renown which is the highest and finest part of national life, will greatly benefit the people of the Philippine Islands, and above all, we will play our part well in the great work of uplifting mankind." Yet, after Roosevelt became president in 1901, his enthusiasm for overseas expansion waned. Urged by imperialists to take over the Dominican Republic, he quipped, "As for annexing the island, I have about the same desire to annex it as a gorged boa constrictor might have to swallow a porcupine wrong-end-to." Under Roosevelt, U.S. colonial holdings shrunk. And after the Russo-Japanese War in 1904–05, Roosevelt changed the United States' diplomatic posture from competitor with the other imperialist powers to mediator in their growing conflicts.

Upon becoming president, Wilson boasted that he could "teach the South American republics to elect good men." After Mexican Gen. Victoriano Huerta arranged the assassination of the democratically elected President Francisco Madero and seized power in February 1913, Wilson promised to unseat the unpopular dictator, using a flimsy pretext to dispatch troops across the border. But instead of being greeted as liberators, the U.S. forces encountered stiff resistance and inspired riots and demonstrations, uniting Huerta with his political opponents. In Mexico City, schoolchildren chanted, "Death to the Gringos." U.S.-owned stores and businesses in Mexico had to close. The Mexico City newspaper *El Imparcial* declared, in a decidedly partial manner, "The soil of the patria is defiled by foreign invasion! We may die, but let us kill!" Wilson learned the hard way that attempts to instill U.S.-style constitutional democracy and capitalism through force were destined to fail.

Wilson drew even more dramatic conclusions about imperialism from the outbreak of the First World War. Like Roosevelt, and many European leaders, Wilson earnestly believed that the rapid spread of imperialism contributed to a higher, more pacific civilization by bringing not only capitalist industry but also higher standards of morality and education to formerly barbarous regions. Sadly, the opposite occurred: The struggle for colonies helped precipitate a savage war among the imperial powers. The only way to prevent future war, Wilson concluded, was to dismantle the colonial structure itself. His plan included self-determination for former colonies, international arms reduction, an open trading system to discourage economic imperialism, and a commitment to collective security through international organizations, what is now sometimes referred to as multilateralism. Wilson never abandoned the evangelical goal of transforming the world, but he recognized that the United States could not do it alone, and it could not succeed overnight—alone or with others. Creating a democratic world could take decades, even centuries, as countries developed at their own pace and according to their own traditions.

After the First World War, Wilson failed to convince either the other victorious powers or the U.S. Senate to embrace his plan for a new world order. During World War II, President Franklin Roosevelt resumed Wilson's attempt to dismantle imperialism. After the war, though, the British and French refused to give up their holdings, and the Soviet Union restored and expanded the older czarist empire in Eastern Europe and Southern and Western Asia. Imperialism endured during the Cold War, but as a subtext of the struggle between the free world and communism.

The Cold War also shaped and distorted the United States' reaction to the powerful movements against imperialism emerging after the Second World War. Fearing that anticolonial movements would side with the Soviet Union, the United States abandoned its effort to dismantle European imperialism, most notably in Southeast Asia, and even sought to establish its own neo-imperial reign in Latin America, Asia, and the

Middle East. The United States did not annex countries. Instead, as it did in Cuba in the early 20th century, Washington sought to dominate these countries' economies and keep friendly governments in power—through quiet subversion or, if necessary, outright military intervention.

The United States' support for ongoing imperial rule led to continuous unrest in the Caribbean and Central America and to disaster in the former French Indochina. The failure to dismantle imperialism was also keenly felt in the Middle East. Since the early 20th century, the great powers had sought control of the region's oil fields. They initially attempted colonization in such countries as Iraq, but failing that, they won favorable long-term leases on the oil fields from pliant governments. In the latter half of the 20th century, the United States continued that pattern. In Iran, for instance, the CIA helped overthrow Prime Minister Mohammad Mossadeq in 1953 in order to restore and sustain the rule of the shah, whom the British installed in 1941. Throughout the region, the United States was considered Britain's imperial successor—a notion reinforced by U.S. support of Israel, which was perceived as an offshoot of European imperialism. (And, after the Six Day War in 1967, Israel itself became an occupying power.) This view of the United States would persist into the next century and frustrate the current Bush administration's efforts to remake the region.

CAVEAT IMPERATOR

With the Cold War over, U.S. Presidents George H.W. Bush and Bill Clinton had the chance to resume Wilson's attempt to dismantle the structure of imperialism that sparked two world wars, the Cold War, and wars of national liberation in Africa, Asia, and Latin America. As both presidents understood, the challenge concerned how the United States could actively exercise leadership—and further America's goals of a peaceful, democratic world—without reviving the perilous dialectic of imperialism and nationalism.

George H.W. Bush met this challenge when Iraq invaded Kuwait in August 1990. If he had acted unilaterally against Iraqi President Saddam Hussein—or solely with Britain, the other former colonial power in the region—the United States would have been regarded as an imperialist aggressor. But Bush wisely sought the support of the United Nations Security Council and created a genuine coalition that included Iraq's Arab neighbors. Clinton followed a similar strategy. In the Balkans, where the collapse of the Soviet empire awakened centuries-old ethnic conflicts, Clinton intervened only as part of a NATO force.

These years represented a triumph of Wilsonianism. Yet, during this period, conservative Republicans challenged Wilson's legacy.

The most vocal dissenters included the second and third generation of the neoconservatives who had helped shape U.S. President Ronald Reagan's domestic and foreign policy. They declared their admiration for the Theodore Roosevelt of the 1890s and the United States' first experiment with imperialism. Some, including Max Boot of the *Wall Street Journal*, called on the United States to unambiguously "embrace its imperial role." Like neo-isolationist and nationalist Republicans, they scorned international institutions and rejected the idea of collective security. But unlike them, neoconservatives strongly advocated using U.S. military and economic power to transform countries and regions in the United States' image.

During the 1990s, these neoconservatives operated like the imperialists of a century before, when Theodore Roosevelt, Sen. Henry Cabot Lodge, and others agitated against the anti-imperialist policies of Democratic U.S. President Grover Cleveland. When McKinley was elected in 1896, Roosevelt joined the administration as assistant secretary of the navy, but the imperialists primarily made their case through speeches, articles, and books. One hundred years later, a like-minded group of neocons, including Wolfowitz, Boot, *Weekly Standard* editor William Kristol, and former Assistant Secretary of Defense Richard Perle, developed a similar network of influence through access to the media. Although they gained only second-level jobs in the new Bush administration, they made the most of them—most notably, by providing an intellectual framework for understanding the Middle East following the attacks on September 11, 2001.

Al Qaeda and its terrorist network were latter-day products of the nationalist reaction to Western imperialism. These Islamic movements shared the same animus toward the West and Israel that older nationalist and Marxist movements did. They openly described the enemy as Western imperialism. Where they differed from the older movements was in their reactionary social outlook, particularly toward women, and in their ultimate aspiration to restore the older Muslim empire to world dominance. But after September 11, as Washington tried to understand what had happened, the neoconservatives insisted that these movements were simply the products of a deranged Islam, inflamed by irrational resentment—in the words of historian Bernard Lewis—of "America's freedom and plenty." The neoconservatives discounted the galvanizing effect that the Israeli-Palestinian conflict and Western power in the region had on radical Islam. And once the Taliban had been ousted from Afghanistan, the neoconservatives set their sights on Baghdad. They argued that the overthrow of Hussein would not only deprive terrorists of a potential ally but could catalyze the transformation of the region into pro-American and pro-Israeli democracies. They denied it would stoke nationalism. Bush, Cheney, Defense Secretary Donald Rumsfeld, and National Security Advisor Condoleezza Rice had earlier denounced nation building, but the neoconservatives, aided by Iraqi exiles, convinced these doubters that Iraq could be transformed on the cheap. In 1899, Manila's upper classes had assured McKinley that he need not worry about "nationalist sentiment." Similarly, in 2003, the neoconservatives and the Iraqi exiles declared that U.S. troops would be welcomed with flowers.

After Baghdad fell in April 2003, and the few flowers had wilted, the Bush administration followed an older script. It put a U.S. administrator in charge of the country. U.S. officials promised eventually to hand sovereignty back to the Iraqis, but they made clear they would do so only after a government was installed that accorded with U.S. interests. It wouldn't be, Rumsfeld assured an interviewer, an "Iranian-type government," regardless of what Iraqis wanted. Even after the handoff of sovereignty, administrator L. Paul Bremer declared the U.S. would retain control. It would be "a sovereign government that can't change laws or make decisions," one Iraqi appointee complained. The Bush administration also declared support for privatizing the Iraqi economy—even though occupying forces are forbidden from selling state assets under the fourth Geneva Convention. (The White House awarded the great bulk of contracts for rebuilding Iraq and its oil industry to U.S. firms.) Ghassan Salamé, a political scientist and former senior advisor to the UN mission in occupied Baghdad, commented in November 2003 that "[t]he Coalition is intent on creating a new Iraq of its own; and one should not ignore the dimensions of that truly imperial ambition."

For his part, Bush declared during an April 2004 press conference that, in invading and occupying Iraq, the United States had not acted as "an imperial power," but as a "liberating power." To be sure, the United States has not attempted to make Iraq part of a new, formal U.S. empire. But the invasion and occupation conformed perfectly to the variant of imperialism pioneered by the United States in Cuba and by the British in the Middle East. Instead of permanently annexing the countries they conquered, after a period of suzerainty, they would retain control by vetoing unfriendly governments and dominating the country's economy.

Predictably, these policies provoked a nationalist backlash. By the spring of 2004, the Bush administration was engaged in a fierce war of urban repression—raining bombs and artillery shells on heavily populated cites—to defend its hold over the country. The president tried to blame opposition to the occupation entirely on foreign terrorists or on high-level loyalists from the old regime, but it is clear that the Iraqi resistance includes people who opposed and even suffered under Hussein's regime.

A BRIDGE TO THE 19th CENTURY

In trying to bring the Middle East into a democratic 21st century, Bush took it—and the United States—back to the dark days at the turn of the last century. Administration officials deeply misunderstood the region and its history. They viewed the Iraqis under Saddam the same way that Americans once viewed the Filipinos under the Spanish or the Mexicans under dictator Huerta—as victims of tyranny who, once freed, would embrace their American conquerors as liberators.

Bush resolved the contradiction between imperialism and liberation simply by denying that the United States was capable of acting as an imperial power. He assumed that by declaring his support for a "democratic Middle East," he had inoculated Americans against the charge of imperialism. But, of course, the United States and Britain had always claimed the highest motives in seeking to dominate other peoples. McKinley had promised to "civilize and Christianize the Filipinos." What mattered was not expressed motives, but methods; and the Bush administration in Iraq, like the McKinley administration in the Philippines, invaded, occupied, and sought to dominate a people they were claiming to liberate.

Neoconservative intellectuals candidly acknowledge that the United States was on an imperial mission, but insist, in the words of neoconservative Stanley Kurtz, that imperialism is "a midwife of democratic self-rule." Yet, in the Philippines in 1900, South Vietnam in 1961, or Iraq today, imperialism has not given birth to democracy, but war, and war conducted with a savagery that has belied the U.S. commitment to Christian civilization or democracy. Abu Ghraib was not the first time U.S. troops used torture on prisoners; it was rampant in the Philippines a century ago. Although nothing is inevitable, the imperial mindset sees the people it seeks to civilize or democratize as inferior and lends itself to inhumane practices. The British used poison gas in Iraq well before the idea ever occurred to Saddam Hussein.

As Iraq descends into violent chaos, some neoconservatives blame the Bush administration for not committing sufficient troops to pacify the population—unwittingly admitting that the neoconservative vision of an Iraq eager for U.S. intervention was mistaken. This kind of heavy hand worked poorly in the Philippines, where U.S. forces had much more firepower than their adversaries, and in Vietnam in the 1960s. But even assuming that an army of 250,000 could have subdued the uprisings in the so-called Sunni triangle and in the Shiite south, would it have altered the fundamental dynamic of imperialism and nationalism and of conqueror and conquered? Or would it have made the brute fact of U.S. domination even more visible to the average Iraqi, and therefore merely delayed, as it did in the Iran of the 1950s, the rejection of all things American?

Americans have always believed they have a special role to play in transforming the world, and their understanding of empire and imperialism has proven critical to this process. America's founders believed their new nation would lead primarily by example, but the imperialists of the 1890s believed the United States could create an empire that would eventually dwarf the rival European empires. The difference would be that America's empire would reflect its own special values. Indiana Sen. Albert Beveridge and the Protestant missionaries advocated "the imperialism of righteousness." God, Beveridge contended, has made "the English-speaking and Teutonic peoples . . . master organizers of the world. . . . He has made us adept in government that we may administer government among the savage and senile peoples. Were it not for such a force as this the world would relapse into barbarism and night. And of all our race He has marked the American people as His chosen nation to finally lead in the regeneration of the world."

By the early 20th century, this vision of American empire had faded, as the United States proved barely capable of retaining its hold over the Philippines. Wilson didn't merely change U.S. foreign policy; he changed its underlying millennial framework. Like Beveridge, he believed the United States was destined to create the Kingdom of God on Earth by actively transforming the world. But Wilson didn't believe it could be done through a U.S. imperium. America's special role would consist in creating a community of power that would dismantle the structure of imperialism and lay the basis for a pacific, prosperous international system. Wilson's vision earned the support not only of Americans but of peoples around the world.

As the 21st century dawned, the neoconservatives adopted Wilson's vision of global democracy, but they sought to achieve it through the unilateral means associated with Beveridge. They saw the United States as an imperial power that could transform the world single-handedly. But the neoconservatives and George W. Bush are likely to learn the same lesson in the early 21st century that Theodore Roosevelt and Woodrow Wilson learned in the early 20th century.

Acting on its own, the United States' ability to dominate and transform remains limited, as the ill-fated mission in Iraq and the reemergence of the Taliban in Afghanistan already suggest. When the United States goes out alone in search of monsters to destroy—venturing in terrain upon which imperial powers have already trod—it can itself become the monster.

"Nations enjoying unrivaled global power have always defined their national interests in increasingly expansive terms," writes Robert Jervis. In the following essay, Jervis expresses dismay at the prospect of the United States falling into a very old and well-laid trap. Empires are prone to reckless extensions of their spheres of control. For the American empire, the current absence of any substantial restraining influence removes the checks and balances that historically reined it in. Long dead are the nineteenth-century European monarchies and the twentieth-century Soviet Union, which both compelled the United States to limit the scope of its imperial activities. The United States, as a consequence, has been freed to pursue its objectives without hindrance, and to enlarge its boundaries without limit. This, in turn, has created conditions that traditionally have led to a fatal arrogance. Empires that have continuously expanding frontiers and no challengers forget that time is against them.

At some point, it follows, an empire becomes too large to sustain itself and collapses under its own weight. In the American case, as Paul Kennedy has famously written, "the United States now runs the risk . . . of what might be called 'imperial overstretch.'"* This fate, imperial mass outgrowing itself, befell ancient Rome, Han China, Ottoman Turkey, and the British Empire, all of which ballooned to immense proportions before caving in on themselves. An insatiable appetite for territory drove each of these empires to conquer or at least to exercise effective control over vast domains. Yet, over time, their holdings became too expensive, in blood and money, to protect and too burdensome to administer. The result in every instance was a catastrophic and permanent imperial retreat. Expansion led inexorably to contraction.

Jervis sees just this fate looming ahead of the United States as it becomes the modern equivalent of the empires of old. America's greatest challenge, therefore, lies not in building its global dominion, but in resisting the temptation to build compulsively.

NOTES

* Paul Kennedy, *The Rise and Fall of the Great Powers: Economic Change and Military Conflict from 1500–2000.* New York: Random House, 1987, 575.

The Compulsive Empire
ROBERT JERVIS

Worried about the aggressive and unilateral exercise of U.S. power around the world today? Fine—just don't blame U.S. President George W. Bush, September 11, or some shadowy neoconservative cabal. Nations enjoying unrivaled global power have always defined their national interests in increasingly expansive terms. Resisting this historical mission creep is the greatest challenge the United States faces today.

The United States today controls a greater share of world power than any other country since the emergence of the nation-state system. Nevertheless, recent U.S. presidents George H.W. Bush and Bill Clinton still cultivated allies and strove to maintain large coalitions. They considered such strategies the best way for the United States to secure desired behavior from others, minimize costs to the nation, and most smoothly manage a complex and contentious world.

By contrast, the fundamental objective of the current Bush doctrine— which seeks to universalize U.S. values and defend preventively against new, nontraditional threats—is the establishment of U.S. hegemony, primacy, or empire. This stance was precipitated both by the election of George W. Bush (who brought to the presidency a more unilateral outlook) and the terrorist attacks of September 11, 2001. Indeed, Bush's transformation after September 11 may parallel his earlier religious conversion: Just as coming to Christ gave meaning to his previously dissolute personal life, so the war on terrorism has become the defining characteristic of his foreign policy and his sacred mission. We can only speculate on what a President Al Gore would have done in the same situation; but while Gore probably would have invaded Afghanistan, he most likely would not have adopted anything like the Bush doctrine.

To some extent, then, the new assertiveness of U.S. hegemony is accidental, the product of a reaction of personalities and events. Yet deeper factors reveal that if this shift in policy was an accident, it was also an accident waiting to happen. The forceful and unilateral exercise of U.S. power is not simply the by-product of September 11, the Bush administration, or some shadowy neoconservative cabal— it is the logical outcome of the current unrivaled U.S. position in the international system.

Put simply, power is checked most effectively by counterbalancing power, and a state that is not subject to severe external pressures tends to feel few restraints at all. Spreading democracy and liberalism throughout the world has always been a U.S. goal, but having so much power makes this aim a more realistic one. It is not as if the Middle East has suddenly become more fertile ground for American ideals; it's just that the United States now has the means to impose its will. The quick U.S. triumph in Afghanistan contributed to the expansion of Washington's goals, and the easy military victory in Iraq will encourage an even broader agenda. The Bush administration is not worried its new doctrine of preventive war will set a precedent for other nations, because U.S. officials believe the dictates that apply to others do not bind the United States. That is not a double standard, they argue; it is realistic leadership.

NIGHTMARES OF A HEGEMON

Great power also instills new fears in the dominant state. A hegemon tends to acquire an enormous stake in world order. As power expands, so does a state's definition of its own interests. Most countries are concerned mainly with what happens in their immediate neighborhoods; but for a hegemon, the world is its neighborhood, and it is not only hubris that leads lone superpowers to be concerned with anything that happens anywhere. However secure states are, they can never feel secure enough. If they are powerful, governments will have compelling reasons to act early and thus prevent others from harming them in the future. The historian John S. Galbraith identified the dynamic of the "turbulent frontier" that produced unintended colonial expansions. For instance, as European powers gained enclaves in Africa in the late 19th century, usually along a coast or river, they also gained unpacified boundaries that needed policing. That led to further expansion of influence and often of settlement, in turn producing new zones of threat and new areas requiring protection. This process encounters few natural limits.

Similarly, the recent wars in Afghanistan and Iraq led to the establishment of U.S. bases and security commitments in Central Asia—one of the last areas in the globe without them. It is not hard to imagine the United States being drawn further into regional politics, even to the point of deploying military force against terrorist or guerrilla movements that arise there, perhaps as a reaction to the hegemon's presence. (The same dynamic could easily play out in Colombia.)

The Bush administration's motives may not be selfish; rather, the combination of power, fear, and perceived opportunity lead it to seek to reshape global politics and various societies around the world. In the administration's eyes, the world cannot stand still. Without strong U.S. intervention, the international environment will become more menacing to the United States and its values, but strong action can help increase global security and produce a better world.

Such reasoning helps elucidate recent international disagreements about U.S. policy toward Iraq. Most of the explanations for the French-led opposition centered either on France's preoccupation with glory and its traditional disdain for the United States or on the peaceful European worldview induced by the continent's success in overcoming historical rivalries and submitting to the rule of law. Or, in neoconservative thinker Robert Kagan's terms, "Americans are from Mars, and Europeans are from Venus."

But are Europeans really so averse to force, so wedded to law? When facing terrorism, Germany and other European countries have not hesitated to employ unrestrained state power the likes of which U.S. Attorney General John Ashcroft would envy, and their current treatment of minorities, especially Muslims, hardly seems liberal. The French disregarded legal rulings against their ban of British beef; they also continue to intervene in Africa and to join other European states in flouting international laws requiring them to allow the import of genetically modified foods. Most European nations also favored the war in Kosovo. Finally, had Europeans suffered a direct attack like that of September 11, it's unlikely that they would have maintained their aversion to the use of force.

The claims of a deep trans-Atlantic cultural divide overlook the fundamental differences between the European and U.S. positions in the international system. U.S. hegemony has three long-term implications that were in high relief during the debate over U.S. action in Iraq. First, only the United States has the power to do anything about a problem like Iraq's Saddam Hussein; Europe faces obvious incentives to free ride in such situations. Second, the large European states have every reason to be concerned about U.S. hegemony and seek to constrain it; they understandably fear a world in which their values and interests are served only at Washington's sufferance. And third, the obsession of U.S. rivals with the role of the U.N. Security Council reflects less an abstract attachment to law and global governance than an appreciation of raw power. France especially, but also Russia and China (two countries that most certainly do not hail from Venus), would gain enormously by establishing the principle that large-scale force can be used only with the approval of the council, of which they are permanent members. Indeed, Security Council membership is one of the major resources at these countries' disposal. If the council were not central, France's influence would be reduced to its African protectorates.

Traditional power considerations also explain why many smaller European countries chose to support the United States on Iraq despite hostile public opinion. The dominance these nations fear most is not

American but Franco-German. The United States is more powerful, but France and Germany are closer and more likely to overshadow them. Indeed, French and German resentment toward such nations is no more surprising than Washington's dismissal of "Old Europe." The irony is that even while France and Germany bitterly decried U.S. efforts to hustle them into line, these two nations disparaged and bullied the East European states that sided with Bush—not exactly Venus-like behavior.

Ultimately, the war against Saddam made clear the links between preventive war and hegemony. Bush's goals are extraordinarily ambitious, involving the remaking not only of international politics but also of recalcitrant societies, which is considered an end in itself as well as a means to U.S. security. The belief of Bush administration officials that Saddam's regime posed an unacceptable menace to the United States only underscores their extremely expansive definition of those interests. The war is hard to understand if its only purpose was to disarm Saddam or to remove him from power—the danger was simply too remote to justify the effort. But if U.S. officials expect regime change in Iraq to bring democracy to the Middle East, to discourage tyrants and energize reformers throughout the world, and to demonstrate the willingness of the United States to ensure a good dose of what the Bush administration considers world order, then the war is a logical part of a larger project. Those who find such fears and hopes excessive would likely agree with the view of British statesman Lord Salisbury, when he opposed intervening against Russia in its conflict with Turkey in 1877–78. "It has generally been acknowledged to be madness to go to war for an idea," he maintained, "but if anything is more unsatisfactory, it is to go to war against a nightmare."

LEAD US NOT INTO INVASION

The United States is the strongest country in the world, yet its power remains subject to two familiar limitations: First, it is harder to build than to destroy. Second, success inevitably depends on others, because even a hegemon needs some external cooperation to achieve its objectives. Of course, countries like Syria and Iran cannot ignore U.S. military capabilities. They may well decide to limit their weapons of mass destruction programs and curtail support for terrorism, as Bush expects. But the prospects for long-run compliance are less bright. Although a frontal assault on U.S. interests is unlikely, highly motivated adversaries will not give up the quest to advance their own perceived interests. The war in Iraq has increased the risks of seeking nuclear weapons, for example, but it also has increased the rewards of obtaining them. Whatever else these weapons can do, they can deter all-out invasion, thus rendering them attractive to any state that fears it might be in the Pentagon's gun sights.

U.S. military strength matters less in relations with allies, and probably also with countries such as Russia, from whom the United States seeks support on a range of issues such as sharing highly sensitive information on terrorism, rebuilding failed states, and managing the international economy. The danger is not that Europe (or even "Old Europe") will counter the United States in the traditional balance-of-power sense, because such a dynamic is usually driven by fears that the dominant state will pose a military threat. Nevertheless, political resistance remains possible, and the fate of the U.S. design for world order lies in the hands of Washington's allies more than its adversaries. Although the United States governs many of the incentives that allies and prospective supporters face, Washington cannot coerce cooperation along the full range of U.S. interests. Perhaps weaker states will decide they are better off by permitting and encouraging assertive U.S. hegemony, which would allow them to reap the benefits from world order while being spared most of the costs. They may also conclude that any challenge to the United States would fail or could incite a dangerous new rivalry.

But the behavior of current and potential U.S. allies will depend on their judgments about several questions: Can the U.S. domestic political system sustain the Bush doctrine in the long run? Will Washington accept allied influence and values? Will it pressure Israel as well as the Palestinians to reach a final peace settlement? More generally, will the United States seek to advance the broad interests of the diverse countries and peoples of the world, or will it exploit its power for its own narrow political, economic, and social interests? Bush's worldview offers little place for other states—even democracies—beyond membership in a supporting cast. Conflating broad interests with narrow ones and believing one has a monopoly on wisdom is an obvious way for a hegemon to become widely regarded as a tyrant.

In his 2000 presidential campaign, Bush said the United States needed a "more humble foreign policy." But the objectives and conceptions of the Bush doctrine point to quite the opposite. Avoiding this imperial temptation will be the greatest challenge the United States faces.

SECTION TWO

The Imperial Present

Republics experience a good deal of anxiety when they find themselves taking on imperial characteristics. They fear that the very label "empire" will slap a stigma on them and force a redrawing of their collective self-image. Such prospects cause uneasiness and often lead a republic to deny that it is becoming an imperial state. By comparison, monarchies and dictatorships transition into empires with far less stress and ideological disruption. In most cases, imperial expansion and administration do not challenge the basic contours of societies that never thought of themselves as republics. The trappings of an empire, in fact, generally suit them rather well. There is no soul-searching, in short, when an autocracy or authoritarian state transforms itself into an empire.

But republics, founded on democratic imagery and institutions, suffer greater trauma in the transformative process. The switch to empire is harder for them. A large part of the reason for this lies in the requirement that a republican society reconsiders and reconfigures its core ideals and values. A republic in the process of becoming an empire must redefine inherited notions of liberty, equality, justice, and civil rights. Uncomfortable compromises must be made, and monumental contradictions must be overlooked. No matter, the end point remains the same. What could be called an imperial republic must acknowledge itself as primarily imperial and put away many cherished myths about who and what it is. Even though it runs counter to many republican beliefs, such a state cannot be, as Niall Ferguson has written, "an empire that dares not speak its name . . . an empire in denial."*

The United States, according to G. John Ikenberry, runs the risk of becoming just that: Ferguson's empire in denial. America, he contends, is drawn toward empire, but it clings tenaciously to its republican identity. This is a prescription for chaos and failure. America's allies and client states expect it to behave like an empire, asserting itself for its own good and theirs. Like Dimitri Simes in a later essay, Ikenberry would have the United States act the part history has apparently assigned it.

NOTES

* Niall Ferguson, *Empire: The Rise and Demise of the British World Order and the Lessons of Global Power.* New York: Basic Books, 2004.

America and the Ambivalence of Power
G. JOHN IKENBERRY

If the last century is viewed as a great struggle between the rule of power and the rule of law among states, the American role in this drama has been paradoxical. As the world's foremost champion of multilateral rules and institutions, the United States also has consistently resisted entangling itself in commitments and obligations. No other country has advanced such far-reaching and elaborate ideas about how rules and multilateral institutions might be established to manage international relations. Yet the United States has been reluctant to tie itself too tightly to such an order—especially recently. Nowhere has this ambivalence about multilateralism and the rule of law been more clearly on display than in the manner of America's invasion and occupation of Iraq. Nowhere, either, are the growing costs of going it alone more apparent.

Across the twentieth century, but particularly at the major postwar turning points of 1919, 1945, and 1989, the United States articulated grand visions of rule-based international order meant to replace or mitigate the balance of power and strategic rivalry. After 1919, America put the League of Nations at the center of its designs for world order; collective security and international law were to provide mechanisms for dispute resolution and the enforcement of agreements. After 1945, the United States came forward with a breathtaking array of new multilateral institutions and rule-based agreements, including the United Nations, the General Agreement on Tariffs and Trade (GATT), the International Monetary Fund, and the World Bank. After the Cold War the United States again pursued an ambitious institutional agenda, including the expansion of NATO and the launching of the North American Free Trade Agreement, the Asia Pacific Economic Cooperation conference, and the World Trade Organization.

At each turn, however, the United States also resisted erosion of its sovereignty and policy autonomy. Its rejections of the League of Nations in 1919, the international Trade Organization in 1947, and, more recently, the International Criminal Court, Kyoto Protocol on global warming, and the Nuclear Test Ban Treaty, offer dramatic evidence of America's reluctance to commit itself to a rule-based international order.

THE NEW UNILATERALISM

Since entering the White House, the Bush administration has articulated a far-reaching skepticism regarding cooperative rule-based relations. Charles Krauthammer, the neoconservative pundit, calls it the "new unilateralism," which "seeks to strengthen American power and unashamedly deploy it on behalf of self-defined global ends."

This new unilateralism is most evident in the Bush administration's rhetoric and policy regarding the use of force. To undergird the fight against terrorism and rogue states that seek weapons of mass destruction, U.S. officials have established an assertive, go-it-alone-if-necessary doctrine. The administration's *2002 National Security Strategy* captures its view on the limits of concerted use of force: "While the United States will constantly strive to enlist the support of the international community, we will not hesitate to act alone, if necessary, to exercise our right of self-defense by acting preemptively against such terrorists, to prevent them from doing harm against our people and our country." Gone are the old justifications of war based on self-defense and imminent threat enshrined in Article 51 of the United Nations charter. America alone will determine when it needs to use force.

In the background of the invasion of Iraq, and emboldened by the 9-11 terrorist attacks on the United States, hard-right policymakers and pundits like Krauthammer have put forward radical new ideas about America's role in the world. These neoconservative thinkers argue for an era of U.S. global rule organized around the bold exercise of unilateral American military power, gradual disentanglement from the constraints of alliances and international rules, and an aggressive push to bring freedom and democracy to threatening countries.

This attitude, exemplified by the Iraq experience but not limited to it, has unsettled world politics. The stakes are high because, in the decade since the end of the cold war, the United States has emerged as an unrivaled and unprecedented global superpower. At no other time in modern history has a single state loomed so large globally. This growth of American power confronts the international community with a frustrating dilemma. The United States has become more crucial to other countries in the realization of their economic and security goals and is increasingly in a position to help or hurt other nations. But America's power also makes it less dependent on weaker states, so it is easier for the United States to resist or ignore them. To other nations, America seems poised between two alternative worlds. In one, the United States continues to build international order around multilateral rules and institutions. In the other, it begins to disentangle itself from international constraints, reverting to a world of power politics where might makes right.

Why is America so conflicted about international rules and laws? Will it, as the world's preeminent global power, retreat even further from a rule-based order to embrace power politics? While some policymakers want to use U.S. supremacy to resist multilateralism and the rule of law, the lesson of history is that even powerful states—and certainly a unipolar America—gain advantage by supporting and operating within an international system of rules and institutions.

THE ROOTS OF AMBIVALENCE

Sovereign states inevitably are of two minds about international order based on the rule of law. The creation of rules and institutions among states offers the promise of peaceful and stable relationships so that governments can conduct their affairs in a more predictable and cooperative environment. But rules and institutions also entail some diminution of a nation-state's sovereign authority and freedom of action. Nation-states are never able or willing to cede full or absolute authority to international rules and agreements, so the international order is always a mixed system where the rule of law and power politics interact.

The simplest explanation for America's ambivalence about rules and institutions is that the country supports them when it can dominate and manipulate them to its advantage, and resists them when it cannot. But a more complex calculation is involved. A rule-based order is attractive to the United States because it locks other states into stable and predictable policy orientations, thereby reducing America's need to use coercion. The United States may be the world's preeminent power, but to rely only on power to get its way is shortsighted and costly. It is much better to persuade weaker and smaller states to operate within a set of rules and institutions that serve the powerful state's long-term interests. Doing so not only reduces the "enforcement costs" that the United States must shoulder to get other states to cooperate, but also "locks in" other states to a framework of cooperation that could last beyond the era of American preeminence.

Still, the United States must pay a price for this rule-based cooperation in the form of constraints on U.S. autonomy and power. In its economic and security ties with East Asia and Europe since 1945, the United States has had to confront a central question: How much policy "lock in" of East Asian and European governments—ensured through multilateral institutions and alliance agreements—is worth how much reduction in U.S. policy autonomy and freedom of action?

RULES THAT BENEFIT THE RULEMAKERS

It is easy to see why the United States sought to build a post-1945 order with multilateral economic and security arrangements organized around the Bretton Woods agreements on monetary and trade relations and the NATO security pact. The United States ended the war in an unprecedented position of power, and the weaker European countries attached a premium to taming and harnessing this newly powerful state. Britain, France, and other major states were willing to accept multilateral agreements to the extent that they also constrained and regularized U.S. economic and security actions. America's agreement to operate within a multilateral economic order and to make an alliance-based security commitment to Europe and Japan were worth the price: it ensured the integration of Japan, Germany, and the rest of Western Europe into a wider U.S.-centered international order.

The mutual benefits of this institutional bargain have been clear enough. The United States has not had to expend its power capabilities to coerce other states, and weaker states have not had to expend resources to protect themselves from a dominating and unpredictable America. The actual restraints on U.S. policy have been minimal. Convertible currencies and open trade have served America's national economic interest. The United States did provide a binding security guarantee to Japan and Western Europe, which rendered U.S. power more acceptable to these countries and left them more eager io cooperate with America in other areas. But the United States did not foreswear the right to unilaterally use force elsewhere. It did agree to operate economically and militarily within multilateral institutions organized around agreed-upon rules and principles. But this also ensured that Japan and Western Europe would be firmly anchored in a global political order that advanced America's long-term national interest.

States within this American-centered order are connected by economic and security relationships informed by rules, norms, and institutions. Participating states accept these rules as a reflection of loosely accepted rights, obligations, and expectations about how "business" is to be done within the order. It is an open system in which members exhibit diffuse reciprocity. Power does not disappear from this multilateral order; it operates in a bargaining system, in which rules and institutions—and power—play an interactive role.

Building on this foundational multilateral order, states have offered and signed a growing number and variety of multilateral agreements. At a global level, between 1970 and 1997, the number of international treaties more than tripled. From 1985 to 1999 alone, the number of international institutions increased by two-thirds. The United States has become party to a growing number of these multilateral contracts. Roughly 150 multilateral treaties included the United States in 1950; the total rose to 400 in 1980 and close to 600 in 2000. The number of multilateral treaties joined by the United States over five-year increments suggests that in the most recent period—from 1996 to 2000—the United States ratified treaties at roughly the same rate as in earlier postwar periods. Measured in these aggregate terms, the United States has continued to increase its institutional connections to the rest of the world.

THE PREROGATIVES OF UNIPOLARITY

Has the rise of America's unipolar power in recent years reduced its incentives to operate in a multilateral, rule-based order? Has the United States become so powerful that it no longer needs to sacrifice autonomy and freedom of action within multilateral agreements? With the end of the cold war and the absence of serious geopolitical challengers, the United States is now able to act alone without serious costs, according to the proponents of unilateralism. If they are right, the international order is in the early stages of a significant transformation, triggered by a continuous and determined effort by the United States to disentangle itself from the multilateral restraints of an earlier era. It matters little who is president and what political party runs the government: the United States will exercise its power more directly, with less mediation or constraint by international rules, institutions, or alliances. The result will be a hegemonic, power-based international order. The rest of the world will complain but other nations will not be able or willing to impose sufficient costs on the United States to alter its growing unilateral orientation.

Many officials in the Bush administration reflect this view. Multilateralism can be a tool or expedient in some circumstances, they believe, but states generally will avoid or shed international and rule-based restraints when they can. Power disparities make it easier for the United States to walk away from potential international agreements. Across the spectrum of policy concerns—from economic and security to environmental issues—the advantages of U.S. power make unilateralism more feasible since the costs of nonagreement are lower for the United States than for other nations. This gives it bargaining advantages if it wants them, but also affords a greater ability to live without agreements and not suffer consequences.

The shifting power differentials have also created a new divergence in interests between the United States and the rest of the world, which further reduces the possibilities for multilateral cooperation. For example, the sheer size of the American economy—boosted by more than a decade of growth unmatched by Europe, Japan, or the other advanced countries—means that U.S. obligations under a Kyoto Protocol to reduce global-warming emissions would have been vastly greater than those of other states.

In the security realm, the United States has global interests and faces threats that no other state shares. America is more likely than other countries to dispatch troops to distant battlefields, which means it would face greater exposure to the legal liabilities of the International Criminal Court. Similarly, the United States must worry about threats to its interests in all the major regions of the world; as the 9-11 terrorist attacks made explicit, American unipolar power makes it a unique target for terrorism. The United States feels itself to be at war while Europeans do not. It is not surprising, therefore, that European and Asian threat assessments about terrorism and rogue states seeking weapons of mass destruction might differ from those of the United States. This growing divergence could make multilateral agreements about the use of force less easy to achieve and less desirable from America's perspective.

NOT GOING IT ALONE

Yet the United States is not structurally destined to disentangle itself from multilateral order and go it alone. There continue to be deep underlying incentives for the United States to support multilateralism and rule-based order—incentives that are growing. These stem from three sources: the functional demands of interdependence, the long-term calculations of power management, and America's political tradition and identity.

American support for multilateralism is likely to be sustained—even in the face of ideological resistance within the Bush administration—in part because of a simple logic: as global economic interdependence grows, the need for multilateral coordination of policies also grows. The more economically interconnected states become, the more dependent they are on the actions of other states for the realization of their objectives. Rising economic interdependence is one of the great hallmarks of the contemporary international system. For more than half a century, states have actively and consistently sought to open markets and reap the economic, social, and technological gains that derive from integration into the world economy. If this remains true in the years ahead, it is easy to predict that demands for multilateral agreements, even and perhaps especially by the United States, will grow rather than shrink.

As the world's dominant country after World War II, America championed GATT and the Bretton Woods institutions to lock other countries into an open global economy that would ensure massive economic gains for itself. But to get these states to organize their domestic orders around an open economy—and accept the political risks and vulnerabilities associated with integration—the United States had to signal that it too would play by the rules and not exploit or abandon these weaker countries. The postwar multilateral institutions facilitated this necessary step. As the world economy and trading system have expanded over the decades, this logic has continued. It is reflected in the World Trade Organization, which replaced GATT in 1995 and embodies an expansive array of legal institutional rules and mechanisms.

In return for the continued support by other states of an increasingly complex international economic system, America must itself become more embedded in this web of rules and institutions. Accordingly, it is not surprising that the Bush administration sought and gained "fast track" authority from Congress to negotiate trade pacts that legislators could not amend when debating ratification, or that the administration led the launch of a new multilateral round of trade talks. Although the recent collapse of trade negotiations in Cancun suggests that agreement on agricultural trade between the advanced and developing worlds is not likely for some years to come, the incentives to search for more open markets remain and will continue to increase.

A second stake that America retains in multilateralism stems from the grand strategic interest in preserving power and creating a stable and legitimate international order. Support for multilateralism offers a way to signal U.S. restraint and commitment to other states, thereby encouraging their acquiescence and cooperation. The United States pursued this strategy throughout the twentieth century—it helps explain the remarkably durable, inclusive, and legitimate character of the existing international order. From this perspective, the search for rule-based agreements should increase rather than decrease with the rise of American unipolarity. The need to manage power effectively with the help of multilateral arrangements will create incentives that will likely limit the Bush administration's unilateral tilt.

THE STRUGGLE OVER IRAQ

The recent struggle between the United States and its security partners over how to deal with Iraq has put American strategic restraint and multilateral security cooperation to the test. Governments around the world were extremely uncomfortable with America's largely unilateral use of force. The Bush administration insisted on its right to act without UN approval, and it ultimately exercised that right. But the decision to seek Security Council support for the war, like the return to the United Nations this fall to ask for help with occupation and reconstruction, implies a growing appreciation for the costs of acting autonomously, if not a preference for placing Iraq policy in a multilateral framework.

It is not surprising that the administration, despite its biases, might be increasingly sensitive to the costs of unilateralism. A chorus of voices from the United States and abroad had warned that the expense in Iraq would be considerable. By going into Iraq largely alone, it was said, America would lack sufficient support after the war for the costly and long-term challenge of rebuilding the country. These warnings have come true. On September 7, President Bush went before the American people to ask for $87 billion in the next fiscal year for the reconstruction of Iraq. This was on top of $54 billion already budgeted. Very soon the cost of the Iraqi occupation will reach a quarter trillion dollars. Congress will provide funding to avoid an even worse disaster in Iraq, but a growing body of opinion insisted that the administration go back to the international community for help to fund reconstruction. Bush's unilateralism is looking increasingly expensive to skeptical Americans.

Beyond the costs involved, the diplomatic struggles over U.S. policy in Iraq also reflect a more general debate about whether agreed-upon rules and principles will guide and limit the exercise of American power. The United Nations Security Council will continue to be a focus of this debate. To bring use of force issues into the Security Council threatens to entangle U.S. foreign policy with the geopolitical agendas of other major states. But the Security Council offers a potential source of legitimacy for American action. The Bush administration wants to protect its freedom to act alone while giving just enough diplomatic ground to preserve the legitimacy of America's global position and garner support for the practical challenges of fighting terrorism. Nation building, however, has proved an increasingly messy as well as expensive business. As a result, calculations of power management compel the administration, almost in spite of itself, to make trade-offs between autonomy and the benefits derived from multilateral cooperation.

SUPPRESSING THE IMPERIAL TEMPTATION

A final source of multilateralism in U.S. foreign policy emerges from the polity itself. America has a distinctive self-understanding about the nature of its own political order, and this has implications for how it thinks about international political order. To be sure, the United States encompasses multiple political traditions that reflect divergent and often competing ideas about how America should relate to the rest of the world. These traditions variously counsel isolationism and activism, realism and idealism, aloofness and engagement in the conduct of foreign policy.

But behind these political-intellectual traditions lie deeper aspects of the nation's political identity that inform the way America seeks to build order in the larger global system.

The United States, from the Enlightenment origins of its founding, has inherited a belief that its political principles possess universal significance and scope. The republican democratic tradition that enshrines the rule of law reflects an enduring American view that polities—domestic or international—are best organized around universally applicable rules and principles of order. America's tradition of civil nationalism also reinforces an orientation that sees the rule of law as the source of legitimacy and political inclusion. This tradition, grounded in national identity, provides background support for a multilateralist foreign policy.

Granted, political leaders can campaign against multilateral institutions and treaties and win votes. America's repudiation of the League of Nations treaty in 1919 constitutes the most dramatic instance among countless examples. Granted, too, the resort to multilateralism is often begrudged or belated. When President Bush went to the United Nations in early 2003 to rally support for his Iraq policy, he did not articulate a central role for the world body in promoting international security and peace. He told the General Assembly that "We will work with the UN Security Council for the necessary resolutions." But he also made clear that the "purposes of the United States should not be doubted. The Security Council resolutions will be enforced . . . or action will be unavoidable."

In contrast, just over a decade earlier, when the elder President Bush appeared before the General Assembly to press his case for resisting Iraq's invasion of Kuwait, he offered a "vision of a new partnership of nations . . . a partnership based on consultations, cooperation and collective action, especially through international and regional organizations; a partnership united by principle and the rule of law and supported by an equitable sharing of both cost and commitment." It would appear that presidents can articulate quite divergent visions of American foreign policy, each resonating in its own way with ideas and beliefs within the American polity. But if this is true, it means that presidents have political and intellectual space to shape policy. They are not captives of what they believe to be a unilateralist-minded public.

Indeed, recent public opinion polls show that the American public is remarkably committed to multilateralism and liberal internationalism. A poll by the German Marshall Fund and the Chicago Council on Foreign Relations found that a majority of Americans favor ratifying the Kyoto Protocol and the International Criminal

Court. When presented with three alternatives about the U.S. role in solving international problems, a clear majority of Americans said that the United States should act to solve problems together with other countries. Only 17 percent agreed that "as the sole remaining superpower the United States should continue to be the preeminent world leader in solving international problems." Americans also strongly support strengthening the United Nations and participating in multilateral peacekeeping operations. Politicians can champion go-it-alone diplomacy, but they are not doing so because the public demands it.

American ambivalence about multilateralism and rule-based international order will not go away, but there are limits on how far the United States can or will remove itself from such an order. A powerful strain of ideology resists the notion of being bound to international rules and institutions. The commanding position of U.S. power today makes these isolationist and unilateralist ideas more influential. The war on terrorism, which leaves the United States feeling vulnerable in new ways, also legitimates these anti-rule-based attitudes. In the background of American foreign policy, an imperial temptation lurks.

Yet, despite these forces and impulses, the United States continues to need an international order organized around rules and institutional cooperation. America cannot achieve its goals without multilateral agreements and institutionalized partnerships. This is why the great drama of the past century persists in the twenty-first, as the United States both resists and rediscovers the international rule of law.

Since the days of Alexander's Greece and Augustus's Rome, military outposts have dotted imperial borderlands. Army garrisons, large and small, have always marked out the farthest reaches of imperial power. These bases, however, have also functioned as economic, social, political, and, above all, cultural crossroads. They represent nodes of contact between the imperial center and a periphery cluttered with colonies, client states, and allies.

Rome, for example, settled army veterans on land near their former posts along the frontier. They enacted this policy for many reasons, not the least of which was in order to reinforce ties to the local population. Discharged and resettled soldiers, in effect, served as flesh and blood conduits between two worlds, between Rome and the outermost fringes of its area of influence. Center and periphery, then, came together in what one writer has described as the nearly permanent "relationship of the frontier soldier to the frontier lands."* Along with merchants and other settlers, Roman soldiers provided the glue that held a vast and diverse empire together.

Similarly, the Han Chinese (202 B.C.–A.D. 220) used their soldiers, stationed in small forts, or "military colonies," in newly acquired territory, as carriers of Han ideas, values, beliefs, and practices. The Han emperors used frontier troops as tools with which to crack open local cultures so that a new Han order could seep in. The soldiers, and others who followed them, could thus make "stealthy progress" toward the "sinicization [transformation into Chinese] of the non-Chinese population."** The later Tang dynasty emperors (A.D. 618–907) elaborated on the Han model. They used a combination of forts, Buddhist monasteries, and commercial towns to transform the famous Silk Road into a cultural and economic superhighway. Tang institutions and customs flowed outward along the Silk Road, creating an integrated, interactive frontier that extended well into Central Asia.

Throughout history, then, military bases have acted as points of contact and exchange between empires and those people and places they influence. The end product is often a mutually beneficial relationship that offers security to the imperial patron while affording protection and prosperity to the outlying client.

As Michael Klare points out in the next essay, this arrangement is alive and well today, except that the imperial patron is the United States and its dependent partners are the former Soviet republics of Central Asia. Klare argues that the United States has stationed its military forces in Eurasia and neighboring parts of the Middle East in order to defend its interests, while establishing close ties with nations in desperate need of protection and trade. It remains to be seen whether or not these forward bases will operate like those of other historical empires, as pipelines carrying American culture far beyond the imperial heartland. It is certain, though, that an American presence will alter the status quo in a very important and volatile part of the world.

NOTES

*   Antonio Santosuosso, *Storming the Heavens: Soldiers, Emperors and Civilians in the Roman Empire* (Boulder, Colo.: Westview Press, 2001), 174.

**   J.A.G. Roberts, *A Concise History of China* (Cambridge, Mass.: Harvard University Press, 1999), 68.

The Empire's New Frontiers
MICHAEL T. KLARE

One of the most striking features of America's emerging military posture is the repositioning of U.S. combat forces from Western Europe and East Asia to a vast region that encompasses the Caucasus, Central Asia, and Southwestern Asia. Before 1990, this area had been virtually free of American military forces. Today, Afghanistan, Georgia, Kyrgyzstan, Pakistan, and Uzbekistan all host American troops and facilities, and the United States provides significant military aid programs to Azerbaijan and Kazakhstan. The United States also has increased its military presence in the Persian Gulf, which abuts this region. Not since the peak of the cold war has a distant corner of the world witnessed such a rapid and substantial buildup of American military power.

The buildup of U.S. forces in this area will have a substantial long-term impact both on regional politics and on relations between the major powers. Long the focus of political and economic competition among China, Russia, and, for a long time, Great Britain, the region will now be roiled by the intrusion of American forces. Because the United States is the newcomer on the scene—the "revisionist power"—it can expect to encounter suspicion and hostility.

It appears, moreover, that the U.S. military buildup in south-central Eurasia will continue in years ahead. The Department of Defense has disclosed plans to restructure America's military presence overseas that will result in a significant shift of U.S. troops from western Eurasia to the south-central region. Describing this move as "the most radical redeployment of American forces since the end of the Cold War," a June 10, 2003, *Wall Street Journal* article reported that it could result in the basing of tens of thousands of U.S. troops in the Caucasus region and Central Asia. Significant numbers of American soldiers may remain in Kyrgyzstan and Uzbekistan long after fighting has subsided in Afghanistan. While U.S. military strength in Iraq likely will decline when the security situation improves or troops from other countries begin to arrive, the United States will no doubt retain a substantial force there as well as in Bahrain, Kuwait, Qatar, and aboard warships in the Persian Gulf itself.

Reflecting this expansion of America's military presence in the region are the growing size and importance of the U.S. Central Command (CENTCOM), the headquarters unit that oversees all U.S. combat forces in the Persian Gulf, Central Asia, and northeastern Africa. Until 1983, the European Command (EURCOM), based in Stuttgart, Germany, and the Pacific Command (PACOM), based in Honolulu, Hawaii, divided responsibility for Central Asia. Both commands viewed the region as lying on the outer, relatively insignificant fringes of their main operational theaters. The 1979 Soviet invasion of Afghanistan and the Islamic Revolution in Iran accorded Central Asia far more importance among U.S. strategists. In what became known as the Carter Doctrine, President Jimmy Carter vowed that the United States would "use any means necessary, including military force" to assure access to the Persian Gulf's critical oil reserves. He also ordered establishment of the Rapid Deployment Joint Task Force, an ensemble of U.S.-based forces available for use in the Gulf area. In 1982, President Ronald Reagan converted the rapid deployment force into CENTCOM, and invested the new command with greater authority. Initially given responsibility over the Gulf region only, CENTCOM has extended its sway to adjacent areas and in 1999 was invested with command authority over U.S. forces and military programs in the former Soviet republics of Central Asia.

As the U.S. military presence in south-central Eurasia swells, the Department of Defense has begun to draw down American troop strength in Germany and other Western European countries. The United States may move some of these forces to the Caucasus, or to new basing facilities in Bulgaria and Romania, which will put them considerably closer to the Caucasus and the Middle East. Reportedly, the Pentagon also plans an eventual reduction in U.S. troop strength in Japan and South Korea, with a corresponding buildup in the South China Sea area. Although they have yet to formally announce any of these moves,

Pentagon officials hint that major troop shifts are likely. "Everything is going to move everywhere," Douglas J. Feith, the undersecretary of defense for policy, remarked this May. "There is not going to be a place in the world where it's going to be the same as it used to be."

A EURASION CHESSBOARD

This shift in military strength from western and eastern to south-central Eurasia will have great significance for the United States and for the major Eurasian powers—including China, India, Iran, Russia, and Turkey—all of which have abiding interests of their own in the area. Indeed, the south-central region could well become, as Berlin and Saigon once were, the new focal point of global geopolitics. Eurasia "is the chessboard on which the struggle for global primacy continues to be played," former national security adviser Zbigniew Brzezinski observed in 1997, and south-central Eurasia likely will prove the main pivot of this struggle. "This huge region, torn by volatile hatreds and surrounded by competing powerful neighbors," will constitute a "major battlefield" in the twenty-first century, Brzezinski predicted in *The Grand Chessboard*.

For most of the powers now seeking advantage on this giant chessboard, south-central Eurasia has long been a site of ethnic warfare and sustained geopolitical rivalry. China's interest in the region goes back to the distant past when it first sought dominion over the great "silk route" connecting Pacific Asia to the Middle East and Europe. The Ottoman Turks and imperial Persia also staked claims to parts of the area. Russia has been a major actor in the region since the early nineteenth century, when czarist rule extended to the Caucasus and Central Asia. In the late nineteenth century, imperial Britain and czarist Russia fought one another and local warlords in the "great game" for regional dominance.

For the United States, south-central Eurasia represented, until very recently, terra incognita. The Defense Intelligence Agency maintained a small electronic listening post in northern Pakistan during the cold war (used primarily for spying on Soviet missile operations in Central Asia), and the Central Intelligence Agency later established supply bases in the same area to provide arms and training to the Afghan mujahideen fighting the Soviet military. Today American soldiers can be found throughout the region, conducting military operations or helping local governments enlarge their own military capabilities. Key U.S. facilities and operations in the region include:

Afghanistan: To coordinate and support continuing operations against remnants of the Taliban and Al Qaeda, CENTCOM has established a joint task force headquarters at Bagram Air Base, outside Kabul, Afghanistan's capital. The United States may abandon other bases in the country when and if combat operations subside, but the Bagram facility likely will remain in U.S. hands for some time to come.

Azerbaijan: As part of a $50 million aid package devised in 2003, the United States is helping Azerbaijan build a small naval force to protect its offshore oil facilities in the Caspian Sea. (The Caspian has been the site of several clashes between Iranian gunboats and international oil company survey vessels.)

Georgia: To help Georgia cope with continuing ethnic violence and protect the vital Baku–Tbilisi–Ceyhan pipeline (a major conduit for the export of Caspian Sea oil to the West), the defense department has embarked on a $64 million "Train and Equip" initiative to enhance the Georgian army's "counterinsurgency capabilities." In 2003, the United States has deployed approximately 150 Special Forces instructors for this purpose.

Kazakhstan: The Department of Defense is helping refurbish an old Soviet air force base at Atyrau on the Caspian Sea's north coast, near the country's Tengiz oil field. According to the Congressional Research Service, rehabilitation of the base is intended "to help Kazakhstan provide security for its energy resources." Once rebuilt, the base also will house a military training center that the United States and Kazakhstan will use for joint training operations.

Kyrgyzstan: The United States has established a forward operations base at Manas International Airport, outside Bishkek, the capital, to support combat operations in Afghanistan. Although initially described as a "temporary" facility, the Bishkek base probably will acquire permanent status as the United States expands its presence in Central Asia.

Qatar: CENTCOM has installed a multibillion-dollar command center to oversee and support combat operations in the Persian Gulf and Central Asia at Al-Udeid Air Base near Doha, Qatar's capital. The command center replaces a similar facility at Prince Sultan Air Base in Saudi Arabia, which the United States mothballed this year in deference to Saudi concerns about the conspicuous American military presence in their country.

Uzbekistan: In return for a mutual defense agreement with the United States, Uzbekistan has granted the Department of Defense use of an old Soviet air base at Khanabad to support combat operations in Afghanistan. Like the facility at Bishkek in Kyrgyzstan, the Khanabad base is expected to remain in U.S. hands after combat operations in Afghanistan have subsided.

Although these developments represent only part of the ongoing military buildup in south-central Eurasia—which also includes a larger naval presence in the Persian Gulf and a growing number of U.S. training missions and combat exercises—they indicate the magnitude of today's global realignment of American combat power. When completed, this realignment will endow the United States with a military infrastructure in the region comparable in many respects to the long-established U.S. infrastructure in Western Europe and the western Pacific. Although less elaborate (and comfortable), America's facilities in south-central Eurasia will be no less capable. Indeed, with the growing U.S. emphasis on a mix of airpower and special operations to defeat hostile forces, the new bases—which are designed with this combination in mind—could prove even more potent than their counterparts in Europe and East Asia.

BEHIND THE REALIGNMENT

What explains the current buildup of American military power in south-central Eurasia? Three factors are paramount: terrorism, oil, and a revival of classical geopolitics.

The groups that pose the greatest terrorist threat to the United States—those associated with Osama bin Laden's Al Qaeda network—remain firmly rooted in the Persian Gulf and Caspian Sea areas. Bin Laden initially established Al Qaeda in the 1980s to fight the Soviet Union in Afghanistan. He later expanded it to combat the perceived enemies of Islam in the Middle East, the Balkans, North Africa, South and Southeast Asia, and eventually the United States. Al Qaeda has recruited combatants from throughout the Middle East and North Africa, as well as from the Arab Islamic diaspora in Europe. Nonetheless, the militant Islamic communities of the Persian Gulf and Southwest Asia continue to provide its primary sources of support. For a time, Al Qaeda enjoyed a secure home base in Afghanistan; with the fall of the Taliban it has relocated to isolated pockets of support in neighboring countries.

Although Al Qaeda remains the primary target of American anti-terror operations, the United States also has acted against other groups with links to that organization or that espouse a similar ideology, such as the Islamic Movement of Uzbekistan and the Abu Sayyef group in the Philippines. The war against terrorism remains centered, however, in the Persian Gulf and Central Asia. To effectively combat terrorist bands, says Andy Hoehn, deputy assistant secretary of defense for strategy, the United States must have a bigger "footprint" in the Middle East and surrounding areas. "If there is a terrorist training camp somewhere and we come to understand that there is something we can do militarily, we don't have a month to do it in . . . . We may only have hours to do it." And this argues, of course, for having bases right in the terrorists' backyard.

Oil is another important factor in the redeployment of U.S. troops. America has long relied on Middle Eastern oil to compensate for a decline in U.S. production. During the first six months of 2003, for example, Saudi Arabia alone provided the United States with 10 percent of its total oil supply, and Iraq and Algeria jointly provided another 4.5 percent. Analysts expect America's dependence on these and other Middle Eastern suppliers to grow as domestic U.S. demand rises and production continues to fall. But the Middle East is notoriously unstable, so Washington seeks to hedge against over-dependence on this region by increasing imports from other areas—especially the Caspian Sea basin.

President Bill Clinton first proposed increased U.S. reliance on Caspian oil in 1997, and the Bush administration has since given it additional emphasis. Indeed, the National Energy Policy (NEP) released by President George W. Bush in May 2001 accords high priority to promoting reliance on the Caspian. The NEP finds "greater diversity of oil production" essential to America's energy security. In this regard, "The Caspian Sea can . . . be a rapidly growing new area of supply." The Caspian basin's estimated total oil reserves—about 30 billion barrels—do not rival those found in the Persian Gulf, but the region holds sufficient untapped petroleum to provide the United States with a vital backup should political conditions in the Gulf result in a significant contraction of supplies.

While attractive as an alternative to the Gulf, procurement of oil from the Caspian region poses significant challenges of its own. The Caspian's five littoral states disagree over the location of offshore boundaries. This has led to periodic naval clashes between the states involved—most notably, between Iran and Azerbaijan—and has discouraged some oil firms from investing in new offshore drilling projects.

Equally problematic, the Caspian Sea itself is landlocked. Petroleum must be shipped by pipeline to ports on a major waterway, such as the Persian Gulf or the Mediterranean Sea. In light of this, the Bush administration has followed a course set by Clinton that favors construction of the Baku–Tbilisi–Ceyhan pipeline from the Caspian to the Mediterranean by way of Georgia and Turkey. Simply obtaining the legal authority and financing for this multibillion-dollar project has proved an enormous challenge for the United States. Now that construction has begun, the United States faces another worry: the pipeline passes through or near six major areas of insurgency and ethnic unrest: Nagorno-Karabakh in Azerbaijan, Chechnya and Dagestan in Russia, South Ossetia and Abkhazia in Georgia, and the Kurdish areas of Turkey. This will make it vulnerable to constant threats of sabotage and attack. In response, the United States is training a special pipeline-protection force in Georgia and providing other affected governments with arms and military know-how. Ultimately, the United States will acquire a cluster of forward operating bases surrounding the Caspian, complementing those already established in Kyrgyzstan and Uzbekistan.

THE REVIVAL OF GEOPOLITICS

Along with terrorism and oil, the perception of new geopolitical challenges and opportunities in Central Asia has proved an impetus for U.S. military expansion in the region. Before World War II, geopolitics—the competitive pursuit of territory, critical resources (water, coal, rubber, oil), and geographic advantage—animated international politics. This drive led to the outward thrust of European imperialism in the seventeenth, eighteenth, and nineteenth centuries, to inter-imperial clashes in Africa and Asia, and eventually to the outbreak of World War I. The rise of fascism and the ideological struggles of the cold war era temporarily eclipsed this sort of geopolitical struggle, but it now appears that traditional geopolitics is being revived. And one of the clearest signs of this revival is the emerging geopolitical rivalry among the United States, Russia, China, Iran, and Turkey in Central Asia and the Caucasus.

Several motivations drive this new competition. Russia once controlled the area as a strategic location at the heart of the czarist and Soviet empires. Now Moscow hopes to extend a sphere of influence over what it calls the "near abroad." Toward that end, it is building ties with the region's authoritarian rulers—many of whom served in leadership positions in the former Soviet Union. Russia's giant energy companies, led by Lukoil and Gazprom, want to exploit the oil and natural gas in the Caspian basin. At the same time, Russia faces serious internal threats from ethnic and religious insurgents in its republics of Chechnya and Dagestan, and so has championed regionwide efforts to combat Islamic extremism. China's interests are roughly parallel. Driven in part by growing needs for imported oil and gas, China also seeks access to the Caspian's vast energy reserves. And, like Russia in Chechnya, China faces a threat from ethnic and religious insurgents in Xinjiang, its westernmost region. For this reason, it, too, seeks to bolster ties with local leaders who face similar insurgent threats. But Moscow and Beijing are also wary of each other's pursuit of influence in the Caspian and Central Asia, and so compete for advantage.

Turkey and Iran, though lacking the military and financial resources available to Russia and China, are also keen to gain influence in the new post-Soviet states in south-central Eurasia. Both have ethnic and linguistic ties to peoples in the region—many of whom speak Turkic or Persian languages—and both see new opportunities, particularly in the energy field. Turkey also hopes to obtain much of its oil and natural gas from the Caspian states, while Iran looks for allies in its ongoing struggle with the United States.

As for the United States, although it wants Russian and Chinese help in the ongoing struggle against Al Qaeda, it is also troubled by Moscow's and Beijing's pursuit of strategic advantage in the region and hopes to minimize their influence. Washington is particularly wary of any move by Russia or China that could jeopardize America's access to Caspian Sea energy supplies. For this reason, the Clinton and Bush administrations have worked tirelessly to ensure construction of the Baku–Tbilisi–Ceyhan pipeline, which will bypass Russia and thus reduce Western reliance on energy conduits that cross through Russian territory (as all existing pipelines from the Caspian do). In the case of Iran, Washington naturally seeks to frustrate Tehran's efforts to gain influence among the Central Asian nations and to play a role in the transport of Caspian oil and gas. (The United States fears that revenues acquired in this manner might help fund Iran's manufacture of nuclear weapons.)

The United States also wants to enhance its own strategic position in south-central Eurasia, much as Great Britain attempted in the late nineteenth century. This effort encompasses anti-terrorism and the pursuit of oil, but many in Washington also see it as an end in itself—as the natural behavior of a global superpower engaged in global dominance. Neoconservatives, who have had a decisive influence on the Bush administration's thinking, in particular hold this view. Precisely because Russia and China—the two most prominent challengers to America's hegemonic status—also seek influence in south-central Eurasia, neoconservatives and their allies in the administration insist that the United States must prevail in this emerging geopolitical contest.

THE REVISIONIST POWER

Most international relations theorists tend to view the United States as a "status quo" power—that is, a nation that enjoys a privileged position in the existing world order and so naturally aims to preserve this order in its current form. A country like China is seen as a "revisionist" power because it seeks to enhance its position relative to the other great powers and so aims to revise or alter the existing world order. Typically, the emergence of a revisionist power is said to constitute a threat to international peace and stability because such powers—Germany before World War I and Japan before World War II, for example—are prepared to take considerable risks in pursuing an enhanced power position.

In south-central Eurasia, however, it is the United States that is the revisionist power, not China or Russia. With the insertion of significant U.S. combat forces, Washington has made itself a major regional actor.

This, in turn, likely will provoke a defensive response by the other regional powers, producing an environment of uncertainty and instability with unpredictable long-term consequences.

That Russia and China view the growing U.S. presence in Central Asia and the Caspian as a threat to their traditional geopolitical interests is undeniable. "It hasn't been left unnoticed in Russia that certain outside interests are trying to weaken our position in the Caspian basin," noted Andrei Y. Urnov of the Russian Ministry of Foreign Affairs in May 2000. "No one should be perplexed that Russia is determined to resist the attempts to encroach on her interests" in the region. Similarly, when it was revealed that the United States intends to retain its "temporary" bases in Kyrgyzstan and Uzbekistan, the speaker of the Russian State Duma, Gennady Seleznyov, warned that "Russia will not endorse the emergence of permanent U.S. military bases in Central Asia." Chinese leaders have been more circumspect in their comments, but there can be little doubt that they feel the same way about the establishment of American bases in China's western backyard.

How will Russia and China respond to the growing U.S. presence? At present, neither seems able or willing to confront the United States head-on; instead, both countries hope to counter American influence by expanding their own diplomatic and economic ties to the new Caspian and Central Asian states. Russia has gone further by offering arms and other forms of military assistance. Russia also stations troops in several of the region's countries (Armenia, Georgia, Tajikistan). It recently expanded its forces in Tajikistan and established a new base in Kyrgyzstan, not far from the U.S. facility at Manas International Airport.

The growing presence of American forces will also provoke a hostile response from ethnic and religious insurgents who are battling U.S.-backed local governments, and from Islamic extremists who oppose U.S. policies on Iraq and Israel. This will produce an unending threat to American soldiers deployed in the region and raise the cost of doing business there And as America's economic and energy interests grow, additional U.S. troops will be needed to protect pipelines and other critical infrastructure.

It is unclear where all of this will lead. The United States, Russia, and China are jockeying for advantage against a regionwide backdrop of instability, insurgency, and terrorism. This could encourage alliances among these three powers, as appears the case today in the war on terrorism; it could also just as easily lead to confrontation and crisis. South-central Eurasia could become the most unsettled and contentious region in world affairs.

S everal earlier authors in this volume have emphasized the fact that the United States fervently denies its imperial condition. To be sure, average Americans, by and large, bristle at the suggestion that their country is an empire. They protest even when confronted with overwhelming evidence of America's past and present imperial ambitions. Americans argue that a democracy, founded in revolution against a parent empire, could not possibly have anything in common with such historical fossils as Achaemenid Persia, Bourbon Spain, and Ottoman Turkey. America, it is claimed, is neither greedy nor repressive and certainly has no designs on free countries overseas. There is no American emperor; rather, a popularly elected president and congress govern the country, and rafts of oppressed American colonies do not clutter world maps. It follows, therefore, that the United States simply cannot be an empire.

Yet, as one observer after another has conceded, in one or more ways America is indeed an empire, albeit an empire that wants to wish away the very power that maintains its global dominance. America seems torn between a persistent republican mythology that emphasizes, as the historian Walter Karp once wrote, a "traditional aversion to colonial empire and overseas dominion" and an undeniably hegemonic reality.* Thus the United States dangles between two extremes, drifting this way and that, missing opportunities to initiate political and social change around the globe. Herein lies America's imperial dilemma: an empire that refuses to admit its true identity unwittingly cripples its ability to project power and further its own interests. An empire like America, as Dimitri Simes writes next, can do little to help itself or the places it dominates if it stubbornly ignores the truth and dodges the responsibilities that come with hegemony. The only solution, according to Simes, is for the United States to acknowledge its imperial character and seize the opportunity to influence world affairs. America is an empire, in other words, and it should act like one.

NOTES

* Walter Karp, *The Politics of War: The Story of Two Wars Which Altered Forever the Political Life of the American Republic.* New York: Harper Colophon Books, 1979, 104.

America's Imperial Dilemma
DIMITRI K. SIMES

THE RELUCTANT EMPIRE

Any realistic discussion of U.S. foreign policy must begin with the recognition that, notwithstanding Americans' views and preferences, most of the world sees the United States as a nascent imperial power. Some nations support the United States precisely because of this, viewing it as a benign liberal empire that can protect them against ambitious regional powers. Others resent it because it stands in the way of their goals. Still others acquiesce to U.S. imperial predominance as a fact of life that cannot be changed and must be accepted.

It is understandable why supporters of the Bush administration's foreign policy balk at any mention of the "e" word. Many past empires were given a bad name not just by their opponents, from national liberation movements to Marxists, but also by their conduct; Nazi Germany and the Soviet Union were the ugliest manifestations. The United States, on the other hand, is said to seek benign influence rather than domination. Its political culture and even its institutional design mitigate against its acting as an effective imperial power. These arguments are not without merit. Still, they reflect more a reluctance to associate American foreign policy with negative imperial stereotypes than a reasoned appreciation of how earlier empires emerged and functioned.

Although empires, like democracies, have taken vastly different forms through history, they have several features in common. First, empires exercise great authority over large and varied territories populated by diverse ethnic groups, cultures, and religions. They rely on a broad range of tools and incentives to maintain this dominance: political persuasion, economic advantage, and cultural influence where possible; coercion and force when necessary. Empires generally expect neighboring states and dependencies to accept their power and accommodate to it. This often contributes to a sense that the imperial power itself need not play by the same rules as ordinary states and that it has unique responsibilities and rights.

Second, empires, more often than not, have emerged spontaneously rather than through a master plan. They frequently evolve as if following the laws of physics; an initial success generates momentum, which is subsequently maintained by inertia. Each new advance creates opportunities and challenges that extend the empire's definition of its interests far beyond its original form.

Ancient Athens, for example, began as the leader of a victorious alliance that defeated the Persians. But it quickly evolved into an empire, against the will of many of its former partners. Thucydides, one of the fathers of realism, describes the Athenian perspective thus: "We did not gain this empire by force. . . . It was the actual course of events which first compelled us to increase our power to its present extent: fear of Persia was our chief motive, though afterwards we thought, too, of our own honor and our own interest."

"Third, empires do not always have sovereignty over their domains. This was certainly the case with Athens. It was also the case in the early period of the Roman Empire, when Rome sought domination rather than direct control over its dependencies. Although some continental European empires, such as Austria-Hungary and tsarist Russia, did establish sovereignty within their territories, other modern empires were less formal, comfortable with enough preponderance to accomplish their political and economic objectives. The Soviet empire, for example, attempted to dominate rather than directly control territories outside of its borders after Stalin's death.

Finally, despite the unpleasant present-day connotations, the imperial experience has not been uniformly negative. Some former empires were agents of change and progress and had generally good intentions vis-à-vis their subjects. The United Kingdom was a prime example of this type, approaching its empire not only with a desire to promote development, but with a self-sacrificing willingness to spend its resources toward that end.

Whether or not the United States now views itself as an empire, for many foreigners it increasingly looks, walks, and talks like one, and they respond to Washington accordingly. There is certainly no reason for American policymakers to refer to the United States as such in public pronouncements, but an understanding of America as an evolving, if reluctant, modern empire is an important analytic tool with profound consequences that American leaders should understand.

Empires cannot escape the laws of history. One of the most salient of these laws is that empires generate opposition to their rule, ranging from strategic realignment among states to terrorism within them. Another is that empires have never been cost free and that the level of opposition to them depends on the costs that the imperial power is willing to shoulder. Both imperial Britain and imperial Rome spent a good deal of time and money quelling unrest and promoting loyalty within their territories. Finally, imperial powers often alter their preimperial forms of government and ways of life. Rome, for example, lost its republican government when it chose to don the imperial mantle. And although the United Kingdom chose democracy over the demands of maintaining its empire, it accumulated substantial immigrant populations from its former colonies, with significant political and economic consequences.

UTOPIAN URGES

An empire that displays weakness and is not taken seriously is an empire in trouble. Being perceived as capricious or imperious, however, is also dangerous. This problem has often occurred when an imperial power insists on imposing a particular vision on the world. How many twentieth-century tragedies were caused, directly or indirectly, in this way? Destiny and choice have made the United States the dominant power in the world today, yet many U.S. policymakers—both Republican and Democrat— have failed to learn from past mistakes. The pursuit of their universal democratic utopia, as attractive as it may seem, is damaging vital U.S. interests and is increasingly coming into conflict with the United States' founding principle of "no taxation without representation."

In the past, a pragmatic foreign policy establishment at home and powerful constraints abroad restrained the United States' messianic instincts. This establishment was built largely around business leaders and lawyers who, although they shared American idealism and a strong sense of the national interest, were cautious and flexible in applying their beliefs to international politics. The Vietnam debacle discredited and divided this group, however, and later demographic and social trends diversified and democratized it. By the 1990s, the pragmatic component in the new foreign policy elite had declined in influence. Instead, powerful but too often reckless single-issue groups and nongovernmental organizations—which aspired to shape policy without having responsibility for its consequences—came to the fore, as did emotional but poorly explained television images.

As a result, American foreign policy moved away from its generally high-minded but interest-based roots to espouse a form of global social engineering. Two illusions facilitated this process: that international crusading can be done cheaply and that those who oppose the United States are motivated by a blanket hatred for American freedom and power, rather than by self-interested objections to specific American actions. These assumptions are simply not accurate, however. A recent major global survey by the Pew Research Center for the People and the Press reveals that those who hold unfavorable views of the United States generally support democratic ideals.

As pragmatism waned, the disintegration of the Soviet Union removed the principal external constraint on U.S. international behavior. The United States' unchallenged military, economic, and political superiority facilitated the view that it could do almost anything it wanted to do in the international arena. In this environment, a new utopian vision was born, the notion that the United States is both entitled and obliged to promote democracy wherever it can—by force if necessary. This idea was enthusiastically promoted in Washington by a de facto alliance of aggressive Wilsonians and neoconservatives, whose apparent belief that the United States cannot settle for anything less than permanent worldwide revolution has more in common with Trotsky than with the legacy of America's forefathers or even the muscular but pragmatic idealism of Theodore Roosevelt.

Typically, the pursuit of moralistic projects has undermined not only American interests but also American values. Double standards and deception, or at least considerable self-deception, have become all too common. For example, U.S. politicians who opposed the International Criminal Court—out of legitimate concern for American sovereignty and fear of politically motivated prosecutions of American soldiers—were simultaneously pressuring the newly democratic Yugoslavia to send its citizens to international war crimes tribunals. Others persuaded the Clinton administration to ignore the UN arms embargo in Bosnia but expressed outrage when other nations violated international sanctions. U.S. politicians across the spectrum have also applied double standards in their approach to foreign campaign contributions: appalled at the notion of another country contributing to the Republicans or Democrats, while insisting that the United States has a duty to fund various foreign political parties, regardless of foreign local laws.

THE CLINTON DOCTRINE

President Bill Clinton's humanitarian and nation-building efforts were a departure from earlier interventions. Defending the Panama Canal or attacking Grenada may have saved innocent lives, but these missions were enacted primarily to serve important American interests or destroy declared enemies. Clinton's moralistic projects, on the other hand, typically were divorced from U.S. interests. Take Haiti, where the United States ousted a nasty, but basically friendly, junta in order to restore to power a nasty, but rather less friendly, President Jean-Bertrand Aristide, who expressed his gratitude by restoring diplomatic relations with Cuba. Or Bosnia, where the Clinton administration cold-shouldered the Vance-Owen partition plan, even though this offered the best hope for a quick end to the bloodshed.

Overall, the results of Clinton's humanitarian interventions were mixed at best. On the positive side, the United States did eventually prevail in Haiti and the Balkans, and it certainly enhanced global perceptions of its power. In addition, U.S.-led interventions probably prevented tit-for-tat killing from spiraling out of control in Bosnia and Kosovo. Yet some of the atrocities that took place were partly the result of the Clinton administration's actions themselves. For example, U.S. policy in the Balkans allowed Croatia to drive 200,000 Serbs from Krajina. It also encouraged Muslims, especially Kosovar Albanians, to pursue radical objectives and reject compromises that, in combination with international pressure, could have averted considerable carnage. To this day, Bosnia and Kosovo remain NATO protectorates, and neither seems prepared to accept the U.S. ideal of interethnic harmony.

Humanitarian interventions also diverted the Clinton admini stration's energy, attention, and resources away from more pressing concerns, such as the growing threat posed by al Qaeda. These mis-directed priorities damaged relations with Russia and, inadvertently, China, complicating efforts to win their cooperation against terrorism in the period before September 11, 2001. Ironically, tension with Russia even contributed to the Clinton administration's rejection of Moscow's proposal to work against the Taliban, offered as early as 1999.

EMPIRE'S NEW CLOTHES

Although September 11 was a wake-up call to American leaders about the dangers of terrorism, too many seem to have drawn the wrong policy conclusions. The principal problem is the mistaken belief that democracy is a talisman for all the world's ills, including terrorism, and that the United States has a responsibility to promote democratic government wherever in the world it is lacking.

The flaw in this approach is not with democracy per se. Liberal democracy with civil society, the rule of law, minority fights, and free but regulated markets is undoubtedly the most humane and efficient way to organize modern society. National Security Adviser Condoleezza Rice is right to point out that suggesting certain people are not interested in freedom or are not ready for democracy's responsibilities is deeply condescending.

It is also condescending, however, to claim that America has the right to impose democracy on other nations and cultures, regardless of their circumstances and preferences. From the Roman Empire to the British Empire, civilization brought on the tips of swords or bayonets has never inspired lasting gratitude. Why should precision weapons be any more effective? As Winston Churchill said, "democracy is the worst form of government except for all those other forms that have been tried from time to time." Treating democracy as a divine revelation—and

Washington as its prophet and global enforcer—simply does not square with the historical record of this form of government, nor with the geopolitical realities of the modern world.

Advocates of the militant promotion of democracy have advanced a variety of questionable arguments to explain why imposing democracy it is not just a moral imperative but an essential practical goal for the United States. One of the most pervasive of these arguments is that democracy will prevent terrorism, since, in the words of former Congressman Newt Gingrich, "the advance of freedom is the surest strategy to undermine the appeal of terror in the world." Recent history suggests otherwise. Even setting aside Islamist terrorists in the United States, how can one explain homegrown terrorists such as radical environmentalists, the Weathermen in the 1960s and 1970s, or Eric Rudolph, recently charged with the Atlanta Olympics bombing? And what about the Irish Republican Army in Northern Ireland or Basque terrorism in democratic Spain?

Another favorite argument is that democracies do not fight one another. But this claim also collapses under scrutiny. If one is willing to consider states democratic by the standards of their time, then there have been several wars between democracies in the past: between Athens and Syracuse, Rome and Carthage, Cromwell's England and the Dutch, and Victorian Britain and South Africa. Moreover, two wars on American soil—the War of 1812 against the United Kingdom and the Civil War itself—were essentially fought between democracies. The reason there were fewer such disputes in the twentieth century was partly because the democracies were united in their struggle against Nazism and communism. With these common enemies gone, however, it is by no means certain that democracies will remain in pacific union. In the Middle East, for example, where popular antisemitic and anti-American feelings abound, democracy could actually increase the probability of conflict between Arab countries and Israel or the United States.

Those who dismiss the idea of conflict between democracies often reject the notion of multipolarity because, in the words of National Security Adviser Rice, "it is a theory of rivalry, of competing interests—and at its worst—competing values." But this position ignores the legitimacy of others' perspectives and would alienate even pro-American democracies if it were to become a principle of U.S. foreign policy. The debate over Iraq demonstrated how little is required for democracies like the United States and France to discover one another's imperfections. Some Russian observers already see recent U.S. administrations as resembling the Soviet Union in their determination to impose homegrown views on others and in their allegedly "Brezhnevite" approach to national sovereignty.

Even if democracy could prevent conflict, it would not guarantee American leadership or even broad support for the United States. In the war against Iraq, for example, democracy was an obstacle to Turkey's support and reinforced, rather than weakened, anti-American policies in France and Germany. On the other hand, the lack of democracy in Egypt, Saudi Arabia, Jordan, and Pakistan allowed those governments to cooperate with the United States, despite hostile public opinion.

Just as democratic nations are not always prepared to support the United States, authoritarian ones sometimes are, including on the crucial issues of our time, such as nonproliferation and terrorism. Driving away such nations—from China to Saudi Arabia—could seriously jeopardize American interests. Obtaining international support for the recent war in Iraq could have been easier if the United States had done a better job in cultivating key partners and regional players.

BREAKING THE BONDS

The United States must be willing to use force, unilaterally if necessary, to protect its security and that of its allies, but it is time for a hardheaded assessment of American interests to play a greater role in Washington's foreign policy calculus. American-led and American financed military interventions for humanitarian ends should in the future be reserved for clear-cut cases of genocide, as took place in the Holocaust, Cambodia in the 1970s and 1980s, and Rwanda in 1994. Otherwise, the United States should engage in humanitarian interventions only with a UN mandate (unlike Kosovo) and, more important, in the certain knowledge that other nations are committed to providing substantial resources.

The Bush administration is correct to argue that the United States should be prepared to do what it takes—including engaging in preemptive action—to pursue terrorists and their sponsors, particularly those seeking weapons of mass destruction. But selective wars of "liberation" are likely to alienate crucial allies. And building constructive relationships with key players, including China and Russia and (as distasteful as it may be to some) Germany and France, is key to success in the war against terrorism and the struggle against WMD proliferation. Thus, although decisive— even ruthless—use of force is appropriate when there is a credible threat, it is important that the United States not use force as a routine instrument of nation building.

Take Iraq. Saddam Hussein's checkered record on WMD, his persistent bullying of neighboring states, his continued violation of UN Security Council resolutions, his support for terrorists, and his attempt to assassinate a former U.S. president revealed him to be a major threat to American interests. Three administrations in a row could not resolve this problem through diplomatic processes. This stalemate justified the U.S.-led invasion last spring. Yet turning Iraq into another American protectorate is less easy to justify, especially when the United States does not possess an international mandate that would increase its legitimacy and defray the mounting costs. Iraq is, predictably, becoming more of a burden than a prize, and the Bush administration would do well to find a formula through which the United States can cede principal responsibility for reconstruction efforts to international organizations while maintaining military control. Acquiring additional burdens by engaging in new wars of liberation is the last thing the United States needs. Even if the U.S. economy improves, such adventures could overwhelm the federal budget, forcing the United States to choose between Roman exploitation—which sowed the seeds of that empire's destruction—and British imperial overstretch—which led to retreat.

The Bush administration's aggressive promotion of democracy also has worrying implications for American interests. As a rule, democratic advancement should be accomplished through the power of example and positive inducement. It is a self-evident fact that being friends with America brings numerous advantages and that the United States prefers to associate with other democracies. This should be incentive enough. Meanwhile, formal unilateral sanctions, which are usually more irritating than punishing, should not be applied as a matter of routine simply to demonstrate U.S. disapproval.

As the indisputable center of power in the world, the United States both benefits from a bandwagon effect and suffers from inevitable foreign backlash. Recent international debates over the U.S. intervention in Iraq demonstrate that although other countries are not prepared to give Washington carte blanche, most are willing to go a long way to accommodate American preferences. American leaders need not shy away from displaying U.S. power assertively, but they must let go of the pretension that the United States is the ultimate font of global wisdom.

Similarly, U.S. leaders must recognize that although rabid anti-American sentiments held in parts of the Muslim world are wholly unjustified, they are partly fueled by a perception of the United States as Israel's uncritical protector. This is not to say that the administration should abandon a staunch ally, nor pressure Israel into fighting terrorism in an unassertive manner. But ending American support for nonessential and provocative Israeli policies—such as its new settlement activity or its refusal to dismantle existing illegal outposts—could have a significant effect on how the United States is viewed in the Muslim world and would probably reduce the appeal of al Qaeda and other extremist groups.

Finally, the United States must address one of its greatest potential vulnerabilities: the combination of empire and immigration. As James Kurth, professor of political science at Swarthmore College, writes, "the conjunction of American empire (America expanding into the world) and American immigration (the world coming into America) has made the very idea of the American national interest problematic. There is a causal connection between empire and immigration, and the two are now coming together as a dynamic duo to utterly transform our world."

It has become increasingly difficult for state and federal agencies to take the tough measures required to regain control over immigration, which has outpaced the absorptive capacity of American society and institutions and is overwhelming the government's ability to enforce crucial immigration laws. No one knows when the United States will reach the point when Balkanization becomes an inevitability. But it is clear from America's current political environment—where single-issue interest groups and true believers in various causes are increasingly able to shape the national agenda—that this point is not very far away. Taking the necessary steps to stop the creeping invasion by illegal immigrants will be controversial and costly. But it is becoming increasingly vital.

Those who criticize the Bush administration for introducing a heavy-handed and unilateral foreign policy miss the mark. There is considerably more continuity between Clinton's interventionism and the current administration's foreign policy than meets the eye. Although candidate George W. Bush said that the United States should be a humble nation and warned against nation building, powerful domestic interests and the shock of September 11 put U.S. foreign policy back onto the track of dangerous imperial overreach: a "one size fits all" approach to democracy promotion fomented under Clinton. A new approach is badly needed, one that exercises power in a determined yet realistic and responsible way—keeping a close eye on American interests and values—but is not bashful about U.S. global supremacy. Only then will the United States be able to take maximum advantage of its power, without being bogged down in expensive and dangerous secondary pursuits that diminish its ability to lead.

The Imperial Future

History and the present state of affairs in the world indicate strongly that the United States exercises a degree of power consistent with empire. That said, America now confronts an age-old question: where to go from the point of hegemony? All empires eventually face this dilemma. They must decide how to proceed after gaining predominance. Options abound. An empire can sit tight, as Rome did after the year 200, consolidating its position and defending what it already has without a great deal of further expansion. It can retreat inward, abandoning some territorial gains, with the intent of protecting the imperial center and limiting contact with the world beyond its frontiers; Ming China (1368–1644) took this route. A mature empire, similar to sixteenth- and seventeenth-century Spain, can switch from conquest to exploitation, from acquiring new territory to removing its wealth. Lastly, an empire can channel its energies from expansion to exporting its cultural traditions, in order to reduce the difficulties and costs of colonial administration. Once the imperial possessions think and act like the center, the empire can turn much of the burden of government over to colonial elites. Great Britain, in varying degrees, opted for this arrangement during the eighteenth century in America and during the nineteenth century in other parts of the world.

These were all attempts to figure out what to do with unrivaled power. This ancient problem should resonate with modern Americans. Their empire, if it properly can be called that, is fast approaching the developmental stage where it will have a surplus of global influence. Many observers, therefore, feel that the United States has reached something of a point of decision. As Richard N. Haass puts it in the following essay, "We're number one. Now what?" The answer, he feels, is self-evident. The United States needs to redesign the world order to reflect a new emphasis on international cooperation and consensus. America, in other words, must craft a cooperative empire of sorts, one that focuses on security, stability, and prosperity. Echoing, in some ways, the recommendations of Dimitri Simes and G. John Ikenberry, Haass urges the United States to assume the leadership role that imperial status confers. America must ensure that the rewards that flow from hegemony benefit every country willing to sign on to its imperial agenda. In constructing this empire of consenting parties, the most useful tools just might be simple persuasion and honest dialogue.

What to Do With American Primacy
Richard N. Haass

WE'RE NUMBER ONE. NOW WHAT?

We live in an era of contradictions: globalization and fragmentation, peace and conflict, prosperity and poverty. Only when one or more of these tendencies wins out will our era gain a name of its own, displacing the awkward "post–Cold War" tag line. But amid this uncertainty is the stark reality that the United States is the most powerful country in the world—first among unequals. Still, this is a description, not a purpose or a policy. The fundamental question that confronts America today is how to exploit its enormous surplus of power in the world: What to do with American primacy?

It must be said at the outset that America's economic and military advantages, while great, are neither unqualified nor permanent. The country's strength is limited by the amount of resources (money, time, political capital) it can spend, which in turn reflects a lack of domestic support for some kind of American global empire. De Tocqueville's observation that democracy is ill suited for conducting foreign policy is even more true in a world without a mortal enemy like the Soviet Union against which to rally the public.

Moreover, U.S. superiority will not last. As power diffuses around the world, America's position relative to others will inevitably erode. It may not seem this way at a moment when the American economy is in full bloom and many countries around the world are sclerotic, but the long-term trend is unmistakable. Other nations are rising, and nonstate actors—ranging from Osama bin Laden to Amnesty International to the International Criminal Court to George Soros—are increasing in number and acquiring power. For all these reasons, an effort to assert or expand U.S. hegemony will fail. Such an action would lack domestic support and stimulate international resistance, which in turn would make the costs of hegemony all the greater and its benefits all the smaller.

Meanwhile, the world is becoming more multipolar. American foreign policy should not resist such multipolarity (which would be futile) but define it. Like unipolarity, multipolarity is simply a description. It tells us about the distribution of power in the world, not about the character or quality of international relations. A multipolar world could be one in which several hostile but roughly equal states confront one another, or one in which a number of states, each possessing significant power, work together in common. The U.S.

objective should be to persuade other centers of political, economic, and military power—including but not limited to nation-states—to believe it is in their self-interest to support constructive notions of how international society should be organized and should operate.

The proper goal for American foreign policy, then, is to encourage a multipolarity characterized by cooperation and concert rather than competition and conflict. In such a world, order would not be limited to peace based on a balance of power or a fear of escalation, but would be founded in a broader agreement on global purposes and problems. In his insightful first book, *A World Restored*, Henry A. Kissinger argues that the competitive multipolar world of nineteenth-century Europe managed to avoid great-power war because the great powers forged a consensus on certain core issues of international relations. American leaders must seek to build such an international consensus for the 21st century.

This goal is not as far-fetched as it may appear. Even now, significant areas of international life are characterized by substantial cooperation, especially in the economic realm. The World Trade Organization (WTO) is an orderly, rule-based mechanism for resolving trade disputes and opening the world economy; finance ministers meet regularly to coordinate monetary policies; and broadly supported conventions ban bribery and corruption. Economic interaction is also regulated by an international marketplace that puts a premium on government policies and procedures—privatization, reduced government subsidies, accepted accounting practices, bankruptcy proceedings—that encourage investment and a free flow of capital.

Military and political interactions are also regulated, although less deeply and extensively. There are some accepted grounds for using military force, such as self-defense. Norms (along with treaties or other arrangements to back them up) outlaw biological and chemical weapons, prohibit nuclear-bomb testing, and discourage the proliferation of nuclear weapons and ballistic missiles. In the political domain, formal international agreements promote human rights, outlaw genocide and other war crimes, and safeguard refugees. Clearly, though, the political-military area is going to be characterized by greater anarchy and discord than is economics. Important questions remain hotly debated: When is it legitimate to use military force other than in self-defense? What should be done to further limit weapons of mass destruction? What restrictions, if any, ought to exist on the ability of governments to act as they wish within their own borders?

Only when there is consensus among the major powers on these and related issues will a significant degree of order exist. Without great-power agreement, international relations could easily revert to a much more hostile system than the one that exists today. With such cooperation, however, we can ameliorate (though never abolish) some of the dangers of great-power competition and war that have plagued the world for much of its history.

FOUR FUNDAMENTALS

Ideally, post–Cold War international society will be built on four foundation stones: using less military force to resolve disputes between states, reducing the number of weapons of mass destruction and the number of states and other groups possessing such weapons, accepting a limited doctrine of humanitarian intervention based on a recognition that people—and not just states—enjoy rights, and economic openness. Such a world would be relatively peaceful, prosperous, and just.

The goal of reducing, if not eliminating, the role of force is not foolishly optimistic. Already, the use of force by one major power against another is either politically unthinkable or prohibitively expensive—with costs that include the danger of escalation to unconventional weaponry. The challenge is to make any such use of force between major powers even more unlikely and to forge agreement about when using force is legitimate.

Real progress has been made in the effort to reduce the role of weapons of mass destruction. The world has come a long way since nuclear weapons were the basic unit of account of great-power competition. U.S. and Russian nuclear inventories are slated to decrease to approximately 3,500 weapons apiece under the signed but (in the Russian case) unratified START II accord. The two inventories would shrink further under START III. Biological and chemical weapons are prohibited, as is all nuclear testing. Although India and Pakistan conducted nuclear tests last year, a number of states, including Ukraine, Belarus, Kazakhstan, South Africa, Brazil, and Argentina, have voluntarily given up nuclear weapons programs in recent years. The remaining items on the agenda include negotiating further reductions in the arsenals of existing nuclear weapons states, principally Russia; methodically introducing defensive antimissile systems; discouraging the proliferation of missile and nuclear capability to additional states or nonstate actors; and enforcing the ban against possessing or using chemical and biological weapons.

The third building block of a post–Cold War world could well prove the most controversial. For 350 years, international order has been buttressed by the notion of sovereignty: that what goes on within the borders of a nation-state is its business and its business alone. The notion of sovereignty was itself an advancement that promoted order by discouraging the meddling that could all too easily lead to conflict. But over the past half century and especially during the past decade, a new reaction against absolute sovereignty has gained strength. Today, sovereignty is increasingly judged as conditional, linked to how a government treats its citizens. When a government proves unable or unwilling to safeguard its citizens—when the inherent contract between the government and the governed is violated—the leadership forfeits its normal right to expect others to keep their distance. It then falls to the international community to act, either diplomatically (utilizing persuasion, sanctions, or aid) or with force, under the banner of humanitarian intervention. The obvious challenge is to gain broader recognition of this modified view of sovereignty, and acceptance of (if not support for) particular interventions.

The fourth building block of post–Cold War international society is economic openness, which requires not only the easy movement of goods, capital, and services across national lines, but also transparent domestic markets that favor private-sector activities. Such openness is necessary to sustain prosperity and works to buttress civil society and increase linkages and interdependencies—factors that should be a bulwark against military conflict. What is needed is not so much a new international financial architecture or added controls on the movement of money as some interior decorating that would increase the transparency and efficiency of national economies throughout much of the world.

BRINGING OTHERS ON BOARD

The world described here will not come about solely from its inherent appeal. To the contrary, building and maintaining such an order requires sustained effort by the world's most powerful actor, the United States. Its ultimate success, in turn, demands that Americans properly handle their country's role as sole superpower of the world. American foreign policy must project an imperial dimension, although not in the sense of territorial control or commercial exploitation; such relationships are neither desirable nor sustainable today. Rather, the United States must attempt to organize the world along certain principles affecting both relations between states and conditions within them. The U.S. role should resemble that of nineteenth-century Great Britain, the global leader of that era. U.S. influence would reflect the appeal of American culture, the strength of the American economy, and the attractiveness of the norms being promoted. Coercion and the use of force would normally be a secondary option.

The United States seeks a world based on peaceful relations, nonproliferation, respect for human rights, and economic openness. It must therefore convince other great powers to join with it to promote these ends, thereby constructing a stronger and more durable order that protects the bulk of U.S. interests and reduces the foreign policy burden—in financial and human terms alike—on the United States.

Certain costs will accompany such a cooperative arrangement. The United States will need to relinquish some freedom of action and modulate the tone of its rhetoric. Sanctions should cease to dominate policy; incentives need to be employed instead, or in tandem. Carrying out unilateral preemptive strikes on suspected weapons facilities, as the United States did in Sudan last August, would become more difficult. The barrier against intervening in internal conflicts would be higher. The pace and extent of additional NATO enlargement would most likely be restrained. The United States would have to limit the scale of any national missile defenses if Russia and China were to cap their strategic forces. Although the benefits would outweigh such costs, bringing about a world that would justify such restraint will be difficult. In fact, three main obstacles lie in the path toward establishing and maintaining an international society to America's liking.

First and most obvious is the opposition of other power centers, major and minor alike. Some resistance is inevitable, at times from France or other European states or Japan, more often from China and Russia. China in particular will oppose any limit on its ability to use force to resolve the Taiwan issue. China is also determined to increase its strategic arsenal. Both China and Russia will feel threatened by American deployment of defensive systems. In response, they may sell technology that could bolster another state's unconventional weapons program. Russia (to some extent) and China (especially) will view humanitarian intervention as a pretext for unwelcome interference in their internal affairs. Japan holds to a more closed view of the ideal economy. Few if any major powers would support preventive attacks on the fledgling unconventional weapons programs of what the United States views as rogue states; as a rule, the United States tends to find itself isolated when emphasizing sanctions and military attacks instead of commerce and other forms of unconditional engagement. A host of smaller but still considerable powers, including India, Pakistan, Iran, Iraq, North Korea, and others, are likely to view an American-led world as discriminatory, threatening, or both.

How, then, might the United States persuade others of the desirability of such a world? The operative word here is "persuade." Areas of consensus will begin to emerge only following strategic dialogues—intense conversations with other governments and opinion leaders in various societies. If *negotiations* were at the center of Cold War diplomacy, *consultations* must form the core of post–Cold War foreign policy. The goal is to build or strengthen global institutions that buttress the basic principles of order. Optimally, this would include a revamped UN Security Council willing and able to counter aggression, whether by one state against another or by a government against its own people; a more comprehensive WTO better able to promote open trade; smaller nuclear arsenals and a reduced chance of nuclear conflict; supplier clubs that restrict the spread of advanced weapons technology; and a stronger International Atomic Energy Agency to police nuclear proliferation and similar organizations to enforce chemical and biological weapons bans.

Why would other states go along with U.S. preferences? In some cases, they will see the same inherent benefits as America. This applies best to Europe, already America's most frequent partner. More generally, economic openness tends to be its own reward. Most major powers also have a stake in avoiding large-scale conflicts, slowing the spread of technologies that threaten them, and maintaining a free flow of oil and gas. Cooperation with the United States will bring benefits in the form of shared technology and capital. At least as important is the status that the United States can confer on its partners. Both Russia and China clearly want to be seen as great powers, as members of the inner circle shaping international relations. Only by working with the United States can they and the UN Security Council avoid being regularly bypassed.

Still, consultations alone—even consultations buttressed by incentives—will not bring about consensus in every area. Persuasion has its limits. The major powers may not agree on general rules; even when they do, they may not agree on how to apply them in a particular situation. In such circumstances, it makes little sense for the United States to work in vain for the emergence of international consensus, guaranteeing only inaction or a lowest common denominator and hence ineffective foreign policy.

The other extreme, unilateralism, likewise has little appeal. On its own, the United States can do little to promote order. Too many of today's challenges—protectionism, proliferation, genocide—cannot be solved by one nation alone, either because cooperation is necessary to combat the problem, resources are limited, or both. The benefits of multilateralism outweigh its tendency to constrain American means and dilute American goals. In addition to distributing the burden of promoting order, multilateralism can restrain the impulses of others, reduce opposition to U.S. actions, and increase the chances of policy success.

What, then, are the options that fall between perfect internationalism and unilateralism? One idea, put forward by Samuel P.

Huntington and others, is dependence on regional powers, sometimes referred to as "pivotal states." There are serious problems with this idea, however. In several regions, the strongest state is not accepted as a legitimate policeman by its weaker neighbors: consider India, Israel, and China. Worse yet, in the Middle East, for example, it is the dominant states (Iran and Iraq) that require policing.

A better option is regionalism. Regionalism is not to be confused with assigning the task of promoting order to regional hegemons. The former involves building consensus and capacity on a regional scale, the latter the assertion of dominance by a single actor over its neighbors.

The problem with regionalism is that in many regions—Northeast Asia, South Asia, the Levant, the Persian Gulf—the principal states do not agree on what constitutes regional order. In other regions such as Europe, the problem is primarily one of capacity. Europe needs far more military muscle—and the ability to speak with a common voice—to play an effective role on the continent or beyond. The same holds for Latin America. In Africa, disagreement and a lack of consensus limit what the principal regional organization (the Organization of African Unity) can do, although subregional organizations have done some good in limited cases.

The main alternative to promoting political, economic, and military order on either a regional or a global scale would be to organize coalitions—as broad as possible—of the able and willing, normally with the United States in the lead. Such groupings are not ideal—they tend to be ad hoc and reactive and lack the legitimacy of UN or formal regional undertakings—but they are consistent with a world where the willingness of governments to cooperate varies from crisis to crisis and situation to situation, and where great-power consensus is unreliable. Lord Palmerston's dictum—"We have no eternal allies, and we have no perpetual enemies. Our interests are eternal and perpetual, and those interests it is our duty to follow"—applies in spades to the post–Cold War world.

INDISCRIMINATE AMERICA

In the end, the creation and maintenance of an American world system will depend as much or more on what Americans and their leaders do as on outside influences. One internal obstacle to properly achieving this goal stems from the desire to do too much, from establishing ends that are overly ambitious. Hegemony, as has already been noted, falls under this rubric. So, too, does democratic enlargement, the only attempt by the Clinton administration to define a post-containment foreign policy doctrine. America simply lacks the means to shape the political culture and system of another country—short of long-term occupation, an option usually unavailable and not guaranteed to work, as demonstrated in Haiti. Moreover, partial success might make countries vulnerable to nationalist fervor. A foreign policy informed by a universal humanitarian impulse would surely qualify as a case of what Paul Kennedy defines as "imperial overstretch." At the same time, not acting entails real costs, not only for the innocent people who lose their homes or lives or both, but also for America's image in the world. Moreover, a narrow foreign policy based solely on self-interest is unlikely to capture the imagination or enjoy the support of the American people, who want a foreign policy with a moral component.

But how can the United States get it right? To address this dilemma, it helps to divide the humanitarian intervention issue into three questions: whether, how, and why to intervene.

What factors should influence the decision to intervene? The first is the scale of the problem: not every repression is a genocide. A second consideration is whether there are other interests, economic or strategic, beyond humanitarianism. Do such interests argue against intervening with military force, as they did in Chechnya, or in favor, as in Bosnia? Third is the matter of partners. How much help can the United States expect from others, militarily and economically? Fourth, what are the likely costs and consequences of intervening? Will action significantly reduce the problem? What larger consequences will acting have for U.S. interests in the region and beyond? Last, what would be the likely results of other policies, including, but not limited to, doing nothing?

Such objective questions are no substitute for situational judgment; there can be no intervention template. But they do provide discipline and, with it, some potential guidance. These considerations would have made the United States less likely to occupy Haiti or expand the Somalia intervention into nation-building, but more likely to act earlier in Bosnia and Rwanda, where a small intervention could have prevented genocide.

It is thus impossible to answer the question of *whether* to intervene without also considering *how* to intervene. The likely costs and benefits of various foreign policy instruments—including diplomacy, political and economic sanctions, incentives, covert action, and military force—need to be weighed. Military options can be further divided to include aiding one side in a conflict, deterring through presence or threats to act, creating safe havens, bombing to weaken or coerce one side, deploying combined armed forces to defeat one or more of the protagonists on the battlefield, nation-building, or sending in forces to keep a peace. Significant interventions that require subsequent long-term occupations cannot be pursued very often.

The third and last question concerns purpose. Humanitarian interventions can be undertaken to prop up a failed state, protect an entire population from danger, or shield part of the populace from the government or another group. If a segment of a society is threatened, when should the United States support the desire of a people for their own state?

A universal bias in favor of self-determination would be destabilizing, so several factors should be weighed. There must be some historical legitimacy. The historical argument can be positive, reflecting a tradition, or negative, resulting from necessity borne of persecution. A second consideration is viability: it makes no sense to encourage independence if the new state would be doomed. A third consideration is internal stability and the likely behavior of the new government toward its citizens. The international community should have done more to condition its support for the independence of parts of the former Yugoslavia on the protection of minorities. A fourth factor is regional stability and the likely reaction of neighboring states. It is for this reason that the United States is correct to oppose a unilateral Palestinian claim for self-determination. Israel has a fundamental stake in this decision. Similarly, Kurdish desires for statehood must be weighed against the claims of Turkey and others. The United States ought not adopt political objectives that are more ambitious than what the humanitarian circumstances warrant.

Inconsistency is unavoidable, but it is also a virtue. Intervening everywhere would exhaust the United States; intervening nowhere would encourage conflict and undermine America's belief in itself and its ability to do good.

What would all this have meant in the case of Kosovo? It is not clear even in retrospect how asking these questions would have influenced the decision to intervene militarily. U.S. interests, while less than vital, went beyond the humanitarian; European allies were prepared to offer significant assistance. At the same time, the scale of the problem was decidedly less than genocide, and strong Russian and Chinese opposition was predictable. The most critical judgment—how to use military force— was one the Clinton administration and NATO got wrong: believing that the threat or use of air power alone would pressure Slobodan Milosevic to cease killing and ethnically cleansing the Kosovars and accept the Rambouillet peace accords. Instead, the bombing turned a humanitarian crisis into something much worse. The fact that 11 weeks of bombing led Milosevic to back down does not alter this judgment. It would have been wiser to continue diplomacy and deal with a limited humanitarian crisis while looking for ways to weaken or topple the Milosevic regime, or to send in ground forces at the outset and prevent the displacement and killing. The administration was correct, however, to avoid making Kosovo's independence an objective, an outcome which would have alienated most European states as well as Russia and led to further regional conflict.

A somewhat restrained approach to humanitarian intervention is unlikely to satisfy either those who wish to place it at the center of American foreign policy or those who wish to relegate it to the periphery. But there must be limits on U.S. military action when a situation is not dire, when partners are scarce, or when other major powers oppose American intervention. Promoting this dimension of world order should not be allowed to undermine the other dimensions. At the end of the day, order is more fundamental than justice; one can have the former without the latter, but not vice versa. Adhering to this precept will take discipline, but discipline is essential in foreign policy if the urgent is not to crowd out the important.

Anyone doubting this assertion need only consider for a moment the costs of a breakdown in any of the other three areas of international order. Major conflict, the spread or use of weapons of mass destruction, or a global financial meltdown would have profound and direct consequences for the United States and American society. Humanitarian abuses simply cannot cause comparable harm on a global scale; as a result, the United States must avoid jeopardizing larger interests when addressing them.

IMPERIAL UNDERSTRETCH

The third obstacle to expanding international order is the opposite of the second. It is the problem of the United States' doing too little, of underachieving. It may seem odd to suggest that a country that spends more than $300 billion a year on national security (if one includes defense, intelligence, economic and military assistance, and diplomacy), stations hundreds of thousands of troops overseas, maintains hundreds of embassies and diplomatic missions of every sort, and listens in on millions of phone calls may not be doing enough, but this is the case. A decade into the post–Cold War era, the United States risks squandering its primacy.

This judgment reflects more than the fact that what is now spent on national security (in terms of percentage of GDP) constitutes a post World War II low. Indeed, it is precisely what we are not prepared to do for our global interests and preferences that is most noteworthy. Examples include an increased unwillingness to commit ground forces and risk casualties; a failure to garner "fast-track" negotiating authority from Congress to expand open trading arrangements beyond NAFTA and the WTO; the low priority given to reducing the U.S. and Russian nuclear arsenals; a half-hearted and arbitrarily limited effort to pressure Iraq into accepting the presence of UN weapons inspectors; a lack of time devoted by senior officials to discussing basic international issues with other powers; and a lack of effort to explain to the American people why they ought to support an active leadership role—indeed, an imperial role—for the United States despite the end of the Cold War and the demise of the Soviet Union.

But no idea, no matter how compelling, ever sells itself. Ideas must compete in the political marketplace. Polls suggesting strong domestic support for U.S. leadership in the world are misleading. They reflect inclination but not intensity; Americans, for the most part, are not so much isolationist—which requires strong feelings about foreign affairs—as disinterested. Polls therefore offer little insight into political behavior or public readiness to sustain foreign policy amid considerable human or financial cost.

The Kosovo experience revealed deep cleavages. And whereas President Clinton has often called for a national dialogue about race, the time has come for a national dialogue on this country's role in the world. Such a dialogue is necessary because what is being argued for here—a foreign policy directed toward promoting world order—demands not only substantial resources but also public attention. Any approach to the world that includes large elements of hegemony and unilateralism will require more than the American public and the U.S. political system can sustain, but the greater danger is that even a multilateral policy of promoting world order will prove to be too much. Future presidents will not be able to appeal to fear as they could during the Cold War. Nor will they have the advantage of simplicity or clarity. Ultimately, the United States will intervene in some crises but not others; other countries will be less than allies but also less than adversaries; and the United States will look differently on other nations' becoming nuclear powers. In this complicated, ambiguous world, greater understanding and explanation will be necessary. Only the president can lead a dialogue on what to do with America's primacy, and this will be a priority for Clinton's successor. "It's the world, stupid" should be his or her refrain.

The fundamental law of gravity applies to empires as it does to everything else on earth—what rises must eventually fall. No imperial state, formal or otherwise, has kept its power forever and unaltered. Their ends, however, have been varied. Some, such as Rome and Han China, collapsed in a historical blink, leaving behind immense power vacuums that took centuries to fill. Others, like the Byzantine Empire and Ottoman Turkey, withered away over time, taking generations to die. Whether it came quickly or gradually, all empires have reached a terminal point where they either shrink down rapidly to an imperial center without a periphery, or progressively decline until they disappear completely.

The fate that history holds in store for the United States is anyone's guess. America could go either way, depending on any number of factors. If the United States expands recklessly, without regard for its domestic well-being, it could buckle under the military and financial weight of its global obligations and give way in a relative instant. If, on the other hand, America does not forcefully pursue an imperial agenda overseas, it runs the risk of stagnation and slow decay. In either case, the future does not look encouraging for the American empire.

There might be one other option, though. The United States might be able to preserve its control over the course of international affairs while shedding the heaviest burdens of imperial rule. Like Richard Haass, Parag Khanna envisions a future in which the United States redefines "empire" as an arrangement that benefits both America and its allies and clients. With such a novel approach, the United States might succeed in defying history. The alternative is to follow its imperial predecessors into oblivion. The United States, put simply, must reposition itself as a benevolent first-among-equals or, as Khanna writes, take center stage in "a replay of an ancient geopolitical tragedy."

The Counsel of Geopolitics
Parag Khanna

During the cold war, geopolitics was synonymous with the U.S.-Soviet struggle for global primacy. But what does geopolitics mean today for our "unipolar moment"? America's overwhelming power inspires outpourings of both self-satisfaction and angst. This national ambivalence should surprise no one, for America's near omnipotence represents equal parts blessing and curse: to enjoy it too easily would be to forget that centuries of history recount—and predict—not just the rise but the fall of great powers. Indeed, if America has reached the apogee of its power, can it go anywhere but downhill from here? Although its expeditious victory in Iraq provoked claims that rumors of America's demise are greatly exaggerated, history demonstrates that aggressive unilateralism only accelerates the inevitable.

"The first and last geopolitical truth is that states pursue security by pursuing power," wrote Michael Glennon recently in *Foreign Affairs*. That truism indeed reflects the geopolitics of all empires past. As the United States extends itself around the world in the name of security— the military is currently active in more than 100 countries—it also falls into the oldest geopolitical trap: imperial overstretch. America may have conquered its geopolitical rivals for now, but averting the fate of empires past will require the defeat of geopolitics itself.

GEOPOLITICS 101

From a beginning that saw it cast as a pseudoscience and the intellectual foundation for Nazi power projection, the field of geopolitics has matured into an analytic synthesis of the past and a prognostic window into the future offering lessons that current policymakers ignore at their peril. One could describe geopolitics as the climatology of international relations, a deep science that uncovers historical cycles and patterns. Since 1982, Charles Pirtle has taught at Georgetown University's Edmund A. Walsh School of Foreign Service, where his students view him—and his course, "Geopolitics"—as both menacing and prophetic. Pirtle's definitions of geopolitics combine the seemingly impersonal forces of geography, environment, economics, and technology with the deeply personal thrusts of human interest and political will. He grins while pointing out that the timeless relevance of the field means that geopolitical scholars, unlike Sovietologists, will never have to apply for jobs in history departments.

Pirtle begins his course with the best-known theory associated with geopolitics, Robert Gilpin's "hegemonic stability theory," which claims that the international system is most stable when there is one dominant power. Over the past thousand years, the mantle of "leading power" has passed steadily westward from the Chinese Song dynasty in the twelfth century to Genghis Khan's Mongol empire, then to the Islamic Mughal dynasty, followed by the Ottomans. Among European great powers, Spain's sixteenth-century monarchy colonized the New World, the seventeenth-century Dutch naval juggernaut ruled world trade, Napoleon's France stretched to Moscow, and throughout the nineteenth century the sun never set on Great Britain's imperium. The twentieth century, of course, brought another westward shift in the locus of global power across the Atlantic to the United States.

Although the United States fulfills the role of hegemon today, it is not too early to speculate whether the inexorable movement of might westward will once again see China as the world's leading power. Indeed, the evolving story of China's growing power is the current incarnation of geopolitics. China had already become in the 1990s a growing concern. Numerous magazine covers envisioned a "new cold war" with the next "evil empire." A controversial Pentagon strategy memo leaked to *The New York Times* pointedly invoked the overarching priority of preventing any great power rivals from emerging. On coming to office; President George W. Bush wasted little time in labeling China "a strategic competitor," a designation that might promote a self-fulfilling prophecy.

BETWEEN CORE AND PERIPHERY

Dipping back into another relevant school of geopolitical thought, Immanuel Wallerstein's "world-system theory" argues that the alternative approach to China—a so-called constructive engagement policy of democracy promotion, increased investment, and economic liberalization—will only expedite China's path to great power status. This prediction flows from a second law of geopolitics: the inevitability of the spread of knowledge and technology between the "core" and "periphery." In other words, globalization itself represents but the acceleration of the world-system phenomenon—bringing, for example, computers and the Internet from America just as it brought printing and gunpowder from China almost 1,000 years ago.

Over time, world-system theory explains, some countries of the periphery will become empowered to climb into the ranks of the core—moving from exploited to exploiting. The relevant corollary, however, holds that as core powers decay, some of them will slip into the periphery. The once mighty Russia, for instance, now is commonly dismissed as "Chad with nuclear weapons." As China builds rail networks to connect with Central Asia, and its population stresses the northern border with Russia (currently suffering an astounding population freefall), one can imagine China eventually controlling what the British geographer

Halford Mackinder called the "geographic pivot of history"—the heartland of the Eurasian "world island."

Within the family of geopolitical theories, methodological strife is set aside for a third common axiom, the "law of unequal growth." It says that the faster economic growth of the hegemon's competitors will diminish the hegemon's edge over its rivals over time, causing unipolar stability to degenerate into power disequilibrium. This is where A. F. K. Organski's "power transition theory" comes into play. Already in the 1960s, geopoliticians recognized China's astonishing power potential as it began to move through the industrial development process. Current trends suggest that the Chinese economy, measured in terms of purchasing power parity, will become as large as the American economy by 2025. Organski's theory predicts that, depending on the rate of the challenger state's power maturation and the degree of friendship between the challenger and the leading state, both sides can prudently avert conflict. Great Britain, for instance, passed the torch after World War I to the vastly more powerful United States in light of their "special relationship." In our own time, however, China's aggregation of land-based power eventually will allow it to deny the United States unfettered command of East Asia's coasts—meaning a showdown over Taiwan, for example, could spark a vast regional conflict.

The next geopolitical apotheosis—involving both the "declining hegemon" America and the "rising regional power" China—is expected between 2025 and 2050. But not only China hawks worry about America's eventual decline from global hegemony. It is worth remembering that 10 years ago, Samuel Huntington's "The Clash of Civilizations?" appeared, arguing that from arms sales and oil pipelines to voting patterns in the United Nations, a Sino-Islamic axis is materializing, heralding America's fall from post–cold war glory. Indeed, to many Americans, on September 11, 2001, fundamentalist Islam became another China literally overnight, a second colossal (and monolithic) menace to national security. The terrorists' ability to lethally strike the homeland, even from within, symbolized to America's enemies a vulnerability of empire to be ruthlessly exploited. Citing both radical Islam (boosted by a Muslim population explosion) and the reawakening Chinese dragon, some conservatives fear that America, like Rome, will be brought down by a combination of hegemonic rivals and technologically empowered terrorists—the new "barbarians" of our age.

Islam is not a geopolitical entity, however, and thus not a great power rival. And although geopolitics tells us that China, India, and perhaps other states will eventually become great powers, it does not teach that World War III several decades from now must inevitably follow. The lessons of geopolitics are intended to challenge historians and political scientists to produce an alternative roadmap that can guide decision makers today, not justify military buildups and preemptive strikes. Even as Pirtle teaches about centuries of historical cycles, he imbues his students with a concern for how American leaders will manage the fact that no empire stays on top forever, and he defies them to thwart the inevitable. On the final day of the course he thunders, "What will you do to prevent this from happening?"

ROME REDUX

Fortunately, America will, for the foreseeable future, shape the rules of world order. Reflecting the sturdiness of America's empire for now, statistics show that the United States spends more on its military than the rest of the world combined, and that America's share of the global economy remains almost one-quarter of the total. Other imperial trappings abound, with the State of the Union address watched and debated around the world, foreign leaders testifying before the Senate, English becoming the dominant language of global communication, and U.S. leadership expected in helping to resolve far-flung disputes.

Yet, despite all this, Americans truly feel their empire is exceptional: unlike the Romans and British, "We don't do conquest." The continuing military occupation of Iraq notwithstanding, historian Niall Ferguson has neatly summed up the U.S. public's stance on imperialism as, "Can we, like, go home now?" Comparing America with his native Britain in the book Empire, he asserts that America considers itself at most an "empire by invitation." Indeed, the United States prefers free-trade agreements to mercantilism, has no desire to colonize the Middle East, and does not plan to relocate the Prime Meridian to pass through New York. Nevertheless, even the most benign of intentions cannot guarantee that America will escape the fate of Rome, especially in the face of deep and growing resentment abroad. As Americans skirmish on the frontiers of empire, they, like the Romans, seem to have willed peace and prepared for war—*Si vis pacem, para bellum*—yet have only seen the latter.

Is the United States itself to blame? A recent sampling of global opinion sums up the answer: no other country in the world likes America's rules. Former South African President Nelson Mandela said a year ago that "the attitude of the United States is a threat to world peace." In May 1999 the Oxford Union submitted this proposition for debate: "Resolved: The United States is a Rogue State." It seems that most people honestly believe the United States wants wars. In a recent BBC survey, only 25 percent of those polled felt that American military power had a positive impact on the world. The geostrategist

Edward Luttwak once remarked that "madness is rare only among individuals; it is quite common in entire nations." Internationally, there is little faith that America will avoid, in a paroxysm of self-righteous madness, plunging the globe into World War III, the first shots of which many believe were fired in Iraq.

According to global poll results, the stakes when it comes to U.S. actions in Iraq or North Korea today involve nothing less than the future international order itself. As America crusades to build world order, others believe America is bent on destroying it. Geopolitical theory defines world order as a "stable distribution of power around the world"; few globally find American hegemony particularly stable. In fact, 40 percent of Russians and French questioned in a Pew survey actually wanted the United States to lose the war in Iraq, dispelling the notion that opposition reflected merely polite disagreement among friends. As the only power with global reach, America's decisions and actions influence other nations' policies and world views. The choice is America's, however, as to whether this influence will be positive or negative, cooperative or conflictual. In its triumphalist hubris, the United States seems to have forgotten that empires are always resented.

IN SEARCH OF MONSTERS

No wonder, then, that America is frequently accused, in the words of John Quincy Adams, of "going abroad, in search of monsters to destroy," or continuously planning, in political scientist Andrew Bacevich's phrase, "Operation 'Insert Name Here' Freedom." Indeed, with Iraq occupied, the targeting of Iran, Syria, and Sudan for "regime change" may already have begun. There is something intellectually seductive, even idealistically appealing, about the notion that if we just "end states who sponsor terrorism," as Deputy Defense Secretary Paul Wolfowitz notoriously put it, the world would be free of existential threats and primed to embrace global cooperation. Yet, as Nietzsche cautioned, "He who would fight monsters must take care not to become one." It is precisely the pursuit of such a chimera that turns the United States into the existential threat it seeks to eradicate. And in a world already chaotic and dangerous, unilaterally applying the hammer of American power in the Middle East and elsewhere almost certainly guarantees the United States another decade of crisis after crisis. While neoconservatives wax philosophical about the benefits of American imperial benevolence, the rest of the world sees the spreading tentacles of exploitative hegemony, fueling resistance and "blowback."

A study earlier this year by the Center for Strategic and International Studies ranks "fear of American dominance" as the number one reason non-nuclear states seek nuclear weapons. The United States discarded the Anti-Ballistic Missile Treaty and has made clear that it has no intention of ratifying the Comprehensive Test Ban Treaty. Both actions indicate a desire to avoid any limits on either its offensive or defensive nuclear options. Whereas treaties provide disincentives for proliferation, America's aggressive counterproliferation doctrine enshrined in the Bush administration's National Security Strategy creates incentives to go brazenly nuclear.

This logic—call it "geopsychology"—reflects the simple, instinctively human suspicion of power. It is the cause of history's arms races, but with a special irony for the United States. Now, even if all nine U.S. naval supercarrier battle groups were to blockade Northeast Asia, an impoverished, cold war holdover like North Korea could still defy and deter the United States with its nuclear weapons. And it would do so claiming self-defense against American encroachment.

Without a greater balance between the uses of American power and how others perceive that power, we can expect America's political bridge heads to continue to sink in the quicksand of the "multitude" of resistance to hegemony evoked by Michael Hardt and Antonio Negri in their neo-Marxist manifesto *Empire*. For all the "soft power" the United States allegedly possesses, the world remains unconvinced that America really does not have imperial pretensions. And if soft power consists of deploying the forces of attraction over coercion, then the United States undercuts its soft power every time it deploys hard power. Meanwhile, other countries already practice "soft balancing," pursuing diplomatic counterweights to overt American bullying. Recall that in 2001 the United States lost its seat on the United Nations Human Rights Committee while Sudan was voted onto the body.

It is ironic that America, the only country in the world with a round-the-clock need to communicate its policies to foreign populations, demonstrates such a large gap in its understanding of the rest of the world. U.S. politicians purchase the power of masterful messaging for their own campaigns but deprive their diplomats of the training and resources necessary, to interact with diverse and demanding audiences around the world. Visible rifts in the transatlantic alliance and within the UN Security Council—over Iraq and global treaties such as the Kyoto Protocol on global warming and the International Criminal Court—underscore the growth of political constraints on America's use of power, portending a broader clash among geopolitical world-views in coming years.

TOYNBEE'S ALTERNATIVE

This imperial hubris, together with the rising multitude of resistance it engenders from other great powers, fundamentalists, and global public opinion, seems like a replay of ancient geopolitical tragedy. History appears to be repeating itself admirably. The question is: Can America's leaders prevent history from turning in its familiar circles—rise and decline, conflict and stalemate—and spur movement toward a collective, self-stabilizing future instead? Fortunately, mankind's geopolitical evolution provides an alternative logic by which the United States could trump history, indefinitely suspending great power rivalries and steering the geopolitical supertanker toward President Woodrow Wilson's 1917 vision of "Not a balance of power, but a community of power, not organized rivalries, but an organized common peace."

The logic of geopolitical evolution underlying Wilson's vision was first articulated by the British historian Arnold Toynbee, who sought to transcend the fatalistic geopolitics of Oswald Spengler's famous Decline of the West. Spengler's two-volume treatise opens with the bold pronouncement, "This book will attempt for the first time to predict history" and goes on to argue that the weakening of a civilization automatically entails the waning—and ultimate disappearance—of its core values (*Kultur*). Toynbee's 10-volume *Study of History* chronicled the extinction of more than a dozen civilizations. But, having witnessed the birth of both the nuclear age and the onset of the cold war, he recognized that this time around, not merely Western civilization, but "Civilization with a big C," was imperiled. In his slender but sweeping 1948 book *Civilization on Trial*, Toynbee asserted that because the West was the first civilization to geographically unify the globe, the geopolitics of unlimited expansion had to be replaced with a new geopolitics for an integrated world. The cold war, rather than dividing the globe, united it in a common geopolitical fate. The transformative potential of Toynbee's evolutionary revelations lies in the imperative to break with an era when states could either expand through conquest or hermetically isolate themselves. Neither is possible today.

Anticipating a world in which nuclear weapons threaten everyone, where rich and poor alike rely on economic interdependence, and major world religions expand and overlap, Toynbee foresaw the need for *Weltinnenpolitik*—a "world domestic politics"—to redefine collective political geography toward the building of a universal community with a common understanding of security. Toynbee proposed a number of principles for governing an integrated world: constitutional, cooperative world government; compromises between free enterprise and socialism; and religious foundations for a secular superstructure. He urged consideration of a longer view, to examine how decisions made today affect not only current events but also future generations, inspiring caution, deliberation, and prudence.

Replacing Spengler's alarmism with foresight, and determinism with agency, Toynbee offered America a choice—an opportunity—that Rome did not have. According to his classic formulation of the stress and response theory, a society can choose either "adaptation" to an integrated world or a "fundamentalism" that remains inflexible to changing conditions. Whereas Spengler viewed decay as an organic force acting on all civilizations, Toynbee argued that, for the first time, civilizations could see the fate that history has in store for them, with the West "relegated to the modest place which is all that it can expect to retain in virtue of its intrinsic worth by comparison with those of other cultures." Great powers, in other words, can adjust. Even though the West, with its liberal, pluralist beliefs, has already been far out-populated by other civilizations, global wars are not inevitable simply because relative decline is.

MAXIMIZING DIMINISHING RETURNS

Today, the critique of the American system so vocally expressed in Europe, Asia, and the Middle East mirrors the ideational threat Toynbee saw posed by communism. In the emerging geopolitical picture, Europe and China will indeed establish their own spheres of influence, diminishing America's decisive role in their affairs, as argues Georgetown's Charles Kupchan, author of *The End of the American Era*. Whether this scenario of "pan-regions"—the United States dominating the Western Hemisphere, Europe calling its own shots, and China holding sway over much of Asia and the Pacific—leads to systemic conflict or a "concert of powers" remains to be seen. Yet it is certain that America, deprived of the powers of persuasion to impose itself on the rest of the world, will be forced to find ways to maximize the diminishing returns on its geopolitical influence. Fifty years after Toynbee's prophecy, can the United States peacefully settle into its "modest place" alongside the world's other great civilizational powers? Communism may have been defeated, with the only proven alternative being some form of market capitalism and constitutional republicanism, but the increased assertiveness of other powers makes extending this system increasingly difficult. It will have to spread itself.

All this suggests that America's "exceptionalism"—its hope of defeating the cycles of history—hinges on using power now to permanently change the rules of the geopolitical game in everyone's favor, including America's own. Yet it is not immediately evident that the United States will define its global role differently from history's other empires, or that it will prove capable of creating long-term stability through a fair division of labor and a harmony of perceptions. Nor is it a given that the same globalization which empowers the enemies of American hegemony—be it China, Islamic fundamentalists, or both— will also facilitate a new global consensus in which a balance of power is not a balance of terror, and where a "clash of civilizations" is averted.

In geopolitics, theory and practice always seem to be chasing each other. In recent years a number of highly respected scholars and intellectuals have expounded on humankind's political future, including Francis Fukuyama (*The End of History*), Michael Mandelbaum (*The Ideas That Conquered the World*), Michael Ignatieff (*Virtual War*), Benjamin Barber (*Jihad vs. McWorld*), Fareed Zakaria (*The Future of Freedom*), Joseph Nye (*The Paradox of American Power*) and, of course, Samuel Huntington. But it is Henry Kissinger—witness to and architect of modern geopolitics—who transcends both the optimism and determinism of others to provide realistic guidance. Already in his first book he cautioned that "Force might conquer the world but it cannot legitimize itself." Instead, as he has recently commented on several occasions, the test of this generation of foreign policymakers is to transform American power to secure a consensus on international norms that protects American values.

In revolutionary times, there is a tendency to repudiate and make a clean break from the past, a pattern that carries increasing danger, particularly if America does not accommodate Chinese and European worldviews into its architecture of world order by making concessions to Europe's preference for a global rule of law and China's guarded strategy toward embracing globalization. The United States should use this critical window of opportunity to reshape global institutions toward greater accountability by sharing burdens and responsibility, but also blame. Doing so would simultaneously raise America's credibility, serve its national interests, and reduce suspicion of the world's only superpower.

In *After Victory*, John Ikenberry argues that—rather than treating alliance partners and other countries like satellites, client states, or protectorates—the United States should act with "strategic restraint," limiting the exercise of its power. It also should use institutions to establish binding commitments, from friends and foes alike, to the "international constitution" that America itself has created. Before resigning from the Bush administration, Richard Haass, a high-ranking State Department official, had been one of the few who spoke of a doctrine of "integration," in which the United States seeks to "build something called an international society . . . [to] get the other power centers in the world"—China, Russia, Japan, Europe, and India—"to sign up to some of the same principles and some of the same goals that we want." But to get other powers on board in building a global concert,

America must submit itself to the same global system of checks and balances, and do so with consistency and continuity.

THE RISK OF SUICIDE

Self-restraint, unfortunately, is not an American virtue. There is no small irony in America's current wavering over a vital global consensus. As Brady Kiesling wrote after resigning in February as political counselor at the U.S. embassy in Athens, "To the extent that international law has utility, it is because we accept it. Neither the world's interests nor our own can be protected without the engagement of the United States, either as first among equals in the evolving law-based international system we largely created, or if, as now seems the case, we are rejecting that system, then as autocrat in whatever system or non-system we replace it with." Yet neither the American government—Democrat or Republican—nor the American people should delude themselves: even for their unique empire, there is no real choice between systems today. Resistance against American power mounts with every step away from the emerging global consensus. If the "universal nation" does not uphold universal values, its world order will eventually collapse. As Toynbee himself wrote, "Great empires do not die by murder, but by suicide."

Surveying the ruins of the *Geopolitik* practiced by Hitler, Germany's first postwar chancellor, Konrad Adenauer, remarked that "history is the sum total of things that could have been avoided." Conscious of the fate of empires past, America now sits uncomfortably in the captain's seat of the global supertanker, facing a choice about which course to follow. If it continues along the present path, the traditional geopolitical predictions of Professor Pirtle's course could prove true. Brian Eno, the enigmatic and brilliant producer of the band U2, best sums up the other path, toward geopolitical evolution: "Isn't civilization what happens when people stop behaving as if they're trapped in a ruthless Darwinian struggle and start thinking about communities and shared futures? . . . Perhaps it's asking a lot to expect America to act differently from all the other empires in history, but wasn't that the original idea?" If America fails to seize this opportunity to choose adaptation over fundamentalism, it will have missed a chance to keep history permanently in the past.

The war in Iraq, to date, has followed a pattern established long ago. As several authors in this volume have noted, America confronted its earliest insurgency in the late nineteenth century following the Spanish–American War. That war, in itself, is redolent of the conflict that in 2003 brought down Iraqi dictator Saddam Hussein. In 1898, the United States provoked a war with Spain with the intention of sweeping the Spanish from the Pacific basin and opening the way for American hegemony in the Far East. It took only a matter of weeks for the United States military to gain a swift victory over a hopelessly outclassed enemy. Much the same occurred a little more than a hundred years later when American power in the Middle East grew at the expense of the corrupt and militarily inferior Hussein regime.

The defeat of Spain and its replacement in the Pacific by the United States announced to the world America's emergence as an imperial player. But the victory, like that in Iraq, soon turned bittersweet. Despite assurances that the United States had no intention of acting the part of imperial overlord, the American government quickly moved to establish an occupation authority in the Philippines. Even before U.S. troops arrived in the islands, the American commanding general was told that "upon the occupation of the islands . . . [he was] to expect from the inhabitants . . . that obedience which will lawfully be due from them."* The Filipinos were to be introduced to a new imperial master. Denied the independence and democracy promised to them by American propaganda, Filipino nationalists rose up and launched a determined insurgent campaign that pitted elusive rebel fighters against tens of thousands of American troops. The bloody contest that ensued raged for three long years, from 1899 to 1902. In many ways, the Philippine Insurrection created the mold, not just for the insurgency in Iraq, but also for the Vietnam War that came between those two conflicts. A dubious justification for war was complicated by vague American aims, no clear definition of victory, and no discernible timetable for the withdrawal of American combat forces. Like Vietnam and Iraq, the contest saw atrocities committed on both sides and a rapid decline in the American public's support for the war effort as the fighting dragged on inconclusively. The Philippines, Vietnam, and Iraq, then, fall neatly into line. It is a historical arrangement that does not bode well for the future of American power today in the Middle East and beyond.

The Iraq conflict and its predecessors share something else in common. During each, American policymakers had little if any idea what to do after the fighting stopped. The next author, Joseph S. Nye,

Jr., makes this very point. He claims that the current administration's objectives in Iraq are muddled, and its priorities are confused. His prescription is a familiar one: The United States should act the imperial part. Iraq, he contends, should serve as a wake-up call for a slumbering empire to sharpen its vision and pursue its goals with greater decision and clarity of purpose. America can reshape global relations and address global problems, but only if it has a sound strategy for doing so.

NOTES

* Walter Karp, *The Politics of War: The Story of Two Wars Which Altered Forever the Political Life of the America Republic*. New York: Harper Colophon Books, 1979, 102.

U.S. Power and Strategy After Iraq
Joseph S. Nye, Jr.

THE VIEW FROM THE TOP

The world is off balance. If anyone doubted the overwhelming nature of U.S. military power, Iraq settled the issue. With the United States representing nearly half of the world's military expenditures, no countervailing coalition can create a traditional military balance of power. Not since Rome has one nation loomed so large above the others. Indeed, the word "empire" has come out of the closet. Respected analysts on both the left and the right are beginning to refer to "American empire" approvingly as the dominant narrative of the twenty-first century. And the military victory in Iraq seems only to have confirmed this new world order.

Americans, however, often misunderstand the nature of their power and tend to extrapolate the present into the future. A little more than a decade ago, the conventional wisdom held that the United States was in decline. In 1992, a presidential candidate won votes by proclaiming that the Cold War was over and Japan had won. Now Americans are told that their unipolar moment will last and that they can do as they will because others have no choice but to follow. But focusing on the imbalance of military power among states is misleading. Beneath that surface structure, the world changed in profound ways during the last decades of the twentieth century. September 11, 2001, was like a flash of lightning on a summer evening that displayed an altered landscape, leaving U.S. policymakers and analysts still groping in the dark, still wondering how to understand and respond.

ABOUT-FACE

George W. Bush entered office committed to a realist foreign policy that would focus on great powers such as China and Russia and eschew nation building in failed states of the less-developed world. China was to be "a strategic competitor," not the "strategic partner" of Bill Clinton's era, and the United States was to take a tougher stance with Russia. But in September 2002, the Bush administration issued a new national security strategy, declaring that "we are menaced less by fleets and armies than by catastrophic technologies falling into the hands of the embittered few." Instead of strategic rivalry, "today, the world's great powers find ourselves on the same side—united by common dangers of terrorist violence and chaos." Not only was Chinese President Jiang Zemin welcomed to Bush's ranch in Crawford, Texas, but Bush's strategy embraces "the emergence of a strong, peaceful, and prosperous China." And it commits the United States to increasing its development assistance and efforts to combat HIV/AIDS, because "weak states, like Afghanistan, can pose as great a danger to our national interest as strong states." Moreover, these policies will be "guided by the conviction that no nation can build a safer, better world alone." How the world turned in one year! And, between the lines, Iraq came to be viewed as the new strategy's first test, even though another member of the "axis of evil" was much closer to developing nuclear weapons.

The rhetoric of the new strategy attracted criticism at home and abroad. The trumpeting of American primacy violated Teddy Roosevelt's advice about speaking softly when you carry a big stick. The United States will remain number one, but there was no need to rub others' noses in it. The neo-Wilsonian promises to promote democracy and freedom struck some traditional realists as dangerously unbounded. The statements about cooperation and coalitions were not followed by equal discussion of institutions. And the much-criticized assertion of a right to preempt could be interpreted either as routine self-defense or as a dangerous precedent.

These criticisms notwithstanding, the Bush administration was correct in its change of focus. The distinguished historian John Lewis Gaddis has compared the new strategy to the seminal days that redefined American foreign policy in the 1940s. Although that comparison may be exaggerated, the new strategy does respond to the deep trends in world politics that were illuminated by the events of September 11. Globalization, for instance, has proved itself to be more than just an economic phenomenon; it has been wearing away at the natural buffers that distance and two oceans have always provided to the United States. September 11 thus dramatized how dreadful conditions in poor, weak countries halfway around the world can have terrible consequences for the United States.

The information revolution and technological change have elevated the importance of transnational issues and have empowered nonstate actors to play a larger role in world politics. A few decades ago, instantaneous global communications were out of the financial reach of all but governments or large organizations such as multinational corporations or the Catholic Church. At the same time, the United States and the Soviet Union were secretly spending billions of dollars on overhead space photography. Now inexpensive commercial satellite photos are available to anyone, and the Internet enabled 1,500 nongovernmental organizations to inexpensively coordinate the "battle of Seattle" that disrupted the World Trade Organization's meeting in December 1999.

Most worrying are the effects of these deep trends on terrorism. Terrorism itself is nothing new, but the "democratization of technology" over the past decades has been making terrorists more lethal and more agile, and the trend is likely to continue. In the twentieth century, a pathological individual—a Hitler or a Stalin—needed the power of a government to be able to kill millions of people. If twenty-first-century terrorists get hold of weapons of mass destruction, this devastating power will for the first time become available to deviant groups and individuals. Traditional state-centric analysts think that punishing states that sponsor terrorism can solve the problem. Such punitive measures might help, but in the end they cannot stop individuals who have already gained access to destructive technology. After all, Timothy McVeigh in the United States and Aum Shinrikyo in Japan were not sponsored by states. And in 2001, one surprise attack by a transnational terrorist group killed more Americans than the state of Japan did in 1941. The "privatization of war" is not only a major historical change in world politics; its potential impact on U.S. cities could drastically alter the nature of American civilization. This shifting ground is what the new Bush strategy gets right.

A STRATEGY DIVIDED

What the Bush administration has not yet sorted out is how to go about implementing its new approach. At first glance, it appears that the Iraq war settled the issue. But the war can be interpreted as the last chapter of the twentieth century rather than the first chapter of the twenty-first. Not only was it unfinished business in the minds of its planners, but it also rested on more than a decade of unfulfilled UN Security Council resolutions. A number of close observers—such as British Ambassador to the UN Sir Jeremy Greenstock—believe that with a little more patience and diplomacy, the administration could have obtained another resolution that would have focused on the sins of Saddam Hussein rather than allowing France and Russia to turn the problem into one of American power. If that close call had come out differently, the continuity with the past would be clearer today. Moreover, the administration is currently faced with another danger-ous dictator who is months rather than years away from having nuclear weapons and thus fits the criteria of the new strategy even more closely than Iraq did. North Korea may prove to be the real test of how to implement the new strategy. Thus far, the Bush administration has responded cautiously and in close consultation with U.S. allies. Deter-rence seems to have worked, although in this case it was North Korea's conventional capacity to wreak havoc on Seoul in the event of war that deterred U.S. military action.

There is also a larger struggle involved in the debate over how to implement the new strategy. The administration is deeply divided between those who want to escape the constraints of the post-1945 institutional framework that the United States helped to build and those who believe U.S. goals are better achieved by working within that framework. The neoconservative "Wilsonians of the right" and the "Jacksonian unilateralists" (to adapt terms coined by historian Walter Russell Mead) are pitted against the more multilateral and cautious traditional realists. The tug of war within the administration was visible both in the strategy document and in the run-up to the Iraq war. Vice President Dick Cheney and Secretary of Defense Donald Rumsfeld disparaged the UN as a "false comfort," traditional realist Republicans such as Brent Scowcroft and James Baker urged a multilateral approach, and President Bush's September 12, 2002, speech to the UN represented a temporary victory for the coalition of U.S. Secretary of State Colin Powell and British Prime Minister Tony Blair. The failure to obtain a second Security Council resolution and the success of the war, however, have ensured the ascendancy of the Jacksonians and the neo-Wilsonians.

Earlier, in 2001, the columnist Charles Krauthammer presaged their vision when he argued for a "new unilateralism," one in which the United States refuses to play the role of a "docile international citizen" and unashamedly pursues its own ends. For most analysts, unilateralism and multilateralism are simply two ends of a spectrum of diplomatic tactics; few leaders follow one or the other approach exclusively. But the new unilateralists go a step further. They believe that today Washington faces new threats of such dire nature that it must escape the constraints of the multilateral structures it helped build after World War II. In their view, the implementation of a new strategy requires more radical change. As Philip Stephens of the Financial Times put it, they would like to reverse Dean Acheson's famous title and be "present at the destruction." They deliberately resisted calling upon NATO after Washington's allies invoked Article 5, offering collective self-defense in the wake of the September 11 terrorist attacks. They sought to minimize the role of the UN in Iraq before and after the war, and they now talk of a "disaggregation" approach to Europe rather than traditional support for European union. In Rumsfeld's words, the issues should determine the coalitions, not vice versa. Some advocates do not shrink from an explicitly imperial approach. In the words of William Kristol, editor of *The Weekly Standard*, "if people want to say we are an imperial power, fine."

ONE-DIMENSIONAL THINKING

Although the new unilateralists are right that maintaining U.S. military strength is crucial and that pure multilateralism is impossible, they make important mistakes that will ultimately undercut the implementation of the new security strategy. Their first mistake is to focus too heavily on military power alone. U.S. military power is essential to global stability and is a critical part of the response to terrorism. But the metaphor of war should not blind Americans to the fact that suppressing terrorism will take years of patient, unspectacular civilian cooperation with other countries in areas such as intelligence sharing, police work, tracing financial flows, and border controls. For example, the American military success in Afghanistan dealt with the easiest part of the problem: toppling an oppressive and weak government in a poor country. But all the precision bombing destroyed only a small fraction of al Qaeda's network, which retains cells in some 60 countries. And bombing cannot resolve the problem of cells in Hamburg or Detroit. Rather than proving the new unilateralists' point, the partial nature of the success in Afghanistan illustrates the continuing need for cooperation. The best response to transnational terrorist networks is networks of cooperating government agencies.

Power is the ability to obtain the outcomes one wants, and the changes sketched out above have made its distribution more complex than first meets the eye. The agenda of world politics has become like a three-dimensional chess game in which one can win only by playing vertically as well as horizontally. On the top board of classical interstate military issues, the United States is likely to remain the only superpower for years to come, and it makes sense to speak in traditional terms of unipolarity or hegemony. However, on the middle board of interstate economic issues, the distribution of power is already multipolar. The United States cannot obtain the outcomes it wants on trade, antitrust, or financial regulation issues without the agreement of the European Union (EU), Japan, and others. It makes little sense to call this distribution "American hegemony." And on the bottom board of transnational issues, power is widely distributed and chaotically organized among state and nonstate actors. It makes no sense at all to call this a "unipolar world" or an "American empire." And, as Bush's new doctrine makes clear, this is precisely the set of issues now intruding into the world of grand strategy. Yet many of the new unilateralists, particularly the Jacksonians, focus almost entirely on the top board of classical military solutions. They mistake the necessary for the sufficient. They are one-dimensional players in a three-dimensional game. In the long term, their approach to implementing the strategy guarantees losing.

SELLING SOFT POWER SHORT

The willingness of other countries to cooperate in dealing with transnational issues such as terrorism depends in part on their own self-interest, but also on the attractiveness of American positions. Soft power lies in the ability to attract and persuade rather than coerce. It means that others want what the United States wants, and there is less need to use carrots and sticks. Hard power, the ability to coerce, grows out of a country's military and economic might. Soft power arises from the attractiveness of a country's culture, political ideals, and policies. When U.S. policies appear legitimate in the eyes of others, American soft power is enhanced. Hard power will always remain crucial in a world of nation-states guarding their independence, but soft power will become increasingly important in dealing with the transnational issues that require multilateral cooperation for their solution.

One of Rumsfeld's "rules" is that "weakness is provocative." In this, he is correct. As Osama bin Laden observed, it is best to bet on the strong horse. The effective demonstration of military power in the second Gulf War, as in the first, might have a deterrent as well as a transformative effect in the Middle East. But the first Gulf War, which led to the Oslo peace process, was widely regarded as legitimate, whereas the legitimacy of the more recent war was contested. Unable to balance American military power, France, Germany, Russia, and China created a coalition to balance American soft power by depriving the United States of the legitimacy that might have been bestowed by a second UN resolution. Although such balancing did not avert the war in Iraq, it did significantly raise its price. When Turkish parliamentarians regarded U.S. policy as illegitimate, they refused Pentagon requests to allow the Fourth Infantry Division to enter Iraq from the north. Inadequate attention to soft power was detrimental to the hard power the United States could bring to bear in the early days of the war. Hard and soft power may sometimes conflict, but they can also reinforce each other. And when the Jacksonians mistake soft power for weakness, they do so at their own risk.

One instructive usage of soft power that the Pentagon got right in the second Gulf War has been called the "weaponization of reporters." Embedding reporters with forward military units undercut Saddam's strategy of creating international outrage by claiming that U.S. troops were deliberately killing civilians. Whereas CNN framed the issues in the first Gulf War, the diffusion of information technology and the rise of new outlets such as al Jazeera in the intervening decade required a new strategy for maintaining soft power during the second. Whatever other issues it raises, embedding reporters in frontline units was a wise response to changing times.

ALLIANCE A LA CARTE

Proponents of the neoconservative strand in the new unilateralism are more attentive to some aspects of soft power. Their Wilsonian emphasis on democracy and human rights can help make U.S. policies attractive to others when these values appear genuine and are pursued in a fair-minded way. The human rights abuses of Saddam's regime have thus become a major post hoc legitimization of the war. Moreover, as indicated earlier, the Bush administration has made wise investments in American soft power by increasing development aid and offering assistance in the campaign against HIV/AIDS. But although they share Woodrow Wilson's desire to spread democracy, the neo-Wilsonians ignore his emphasis on institutions. In the absence of international institutions through which others can feel consulted and involved, the imperial imposition of values may neither attract others nor produce soft power.

Both the neo-Wilsonian and the Jacksonian strands of the new unilateralism tend to prefer alliance à la carte and to treat international institutions as toolboxes into which U.S. policymakers can reach when convenient. But this approach neglects the ways in which institutions legitimize disproportionate American power. When others feel that they have been consulted, they are more likely to be helpful. For example, NATO members are doing much of the work of keeping the peace in the Balkans and in Afghanistan. NATO works through many committees to achieve the standardization and interoperability that allow coalitions of the willing to be more than ad hoc groupings. Without regular institutional consultation, the United States may find others increasingly reluctant to put tools into the toolbox. One day the box might even be bare. American-led coalitions will become less willing and shrink in size—witness the two gulf wars.

The UN is a particularly difficult institution. The power of the veto in the Security Council has prevented it from authorizing the use of force for collective-security operations in all but three cases in the past half-century. But the council was specifically designed to be a concert of large powers that would not work when they disagreed. The veto is like a fuse box in the electrical system of a house. Better that a fuse blows and the lights go out than that the house burns down. Moreover, as UN Secretary-General Kofi Annan pointed out after the Kosovo war proceeded in 1999 without a UN resolution—but with French and German participation—the UN is torn between the strict Westphalian interpretation of state sovereignty and the rise of international humanitarian and human rights law that sets limits on what leaders can do to their citizens. To complicate matters further, politics has made the UN Charter virtually impossible to amend. Still, for all its flaws, the UN has proved useful in its humanitarian and peacekeeping roles on which states agree, and it remains an important source of legitimacy in world politics.

The latter point is particularly galling to the new unilateralists, who (correctly) point to the undemocratic nature of many of the regimes that cast votes in the UN and chair its committees—one rankling example being Libya's chairmanship of the Human Rights Commission. But their proposed solution of replacing the UN with a new organization of democracies ignores the fact that the major divisions over Iraq were among the democracies. Rather than engage in futile efforts to ignore the UN or change its architecture, Washington should improve its underlying bilateral diplomacy with the other veto-wielding powers and use the UN in practical ways to further the new strategy. In addition to overseeing the UN's development and humanitarian agenda, the Security Council may wind up playing a background role in diffusing the crisis in North Korea; the Committee on Terrorism can help prod states to improve their procedures; and UN peacekeepers can save the United States from having to be the world's lone sheriff. If Washington uses it wisely, the UN can serve U.S. interests in a variety of practical ways. But the reverse is also true: the new unilateralists' attacks on the UN may backfire in ways that undercut American soft power.

There is considerable evidence that the new unilateralists' policies tend to squander U.S. soft power. Before the war, a Pew Charitable Trust poll found that U.S. policies (not American culture) led to less favorable attitudes toward the United States over the past two years in 19 of 27 countries, including the Islamic countries so crucial to the prosecution of the war on terrorism. Other polls showed an average drop of 30 points in the popularity of the United States in major European countries.

No large country can afford to be purely multilateralist, and sometimes the United States must take the lead by itself, as it did in Afghanistan. And the credible threat to exercise the unilateral option was probably essential to getting the UN Security Council to pass Resolution 1441, which brought the weapons inspectors back into Iraq. But the United States should incline toward multilateralism whenever possible as a way to legitimize its power and to gain broad acceptance of its new strategy. Preemption that is legitimized by multilateral sanction is far less costly and sets a far less dangerous precedent than the United States asserting that it alone can act as judge, jury, and executioner. Granted, multilateralism can be used by smaller states to restrict American freedom of action, but this downside does not detract from its overall usefulness. Whether Washington learns to listen to others and to define U.S. national interests more broadly to include global interests will be crucial to the success of the new strategy and to whether others see the American preponderance the strategy proclaims as benign or not. To implement the new strategy successfully, therefore, the United States will need to pay more attention to soft power and multilateral cooperation than the new unilateralists would like.

IMPERIAL UNDERSTRETCH

Finally, those of the new unilateralists who openly welcome the idea of an American empire mistake the underlying nature of American public opinion. Even if the transformation of undemocratic regimes in the Middle East would indeed reduce some of the sources of Islamic terrorism, the question remains whether the American public will tolerate an imperial role. Neoconservative writers such as Max Boot argue that the United States should provide troubled countries with "the sort of enlightened foreign administration once provided by self-confident Englishmen in jodhpurs and pith helmets," but as the British historian Niall Ferguson points out, modern America differs from nineteenth-century Britain in its chronically short attention span.

Some say the United States is already an empire and it is just a matter of recognizing reality, but they mistake the politics of primacy for those of empire. The United States may be more powerful compared to other countries than the United Kingdom was at its imperial peak, but it has less control over what occurs inside other countries than the United Kingdom did when it ruled a quarter of the globe. For example, Kenya's schools, taxes, laws, and elections—not to mention external relations—were controlled by British officials. The United States has no such control over any country today. Washington could not even get the votes of Mexico City and Santiago for a second Security Council resolution. Devotees of the new imperialism argue that such analysis is too literal, that "empire" is intended merely as a metaphor. But this "metaphor" implies a control from Washington that is unrealistic and reinforces the prevailing temptations of unilateralism.

Despite its natal ideology of anti-imperialism, the United States has intervened and governed countries in Central America and the Caribbean, as well as the Philippines. But Americans have never felt comfortable as imperialists, and only a small number of cases led directly to the establishment of democracies. American empire is not limited by "imperial overstretch" in the sense of costing an unsustainable portion of U.S. gross domestic product. Indeed, the United States devoted a much higher percentage of GDP to the military budget during the Cold War than it does today. The overstretch will come from having to police more peripheral countries than public opinion will accept. Even after the second Gulf War, polls show little taste for empire and no public inclination toward invading Syria and Iran. Instead, the American public continues to say that it favors multilateralism and using the UN.

In fact, the problem of creating an American empire might better be termed "imperial understretch." Neither the public nor Congress has proved willing to invest seriously in the instruments of nation building and governance, as opposed to military force. The entire allotment for the State Department and the U.S. Agency for International Development is only 1 percent of the federal budget. The United States spends nearly 16 times as much on its military, and there is little indication of change to come in this era of tax cuts and budget deficits. The U.S. military is designed for fighting rather than police work, and the Pentagon has cut back on training for peacekeeping operations. In practice, the coalition of neo-Wilsonians and Jacksonians may divide over this issue. The former will espouse a prolonged U.S. presence to produce democracy in the Middle East, whereas the latter, who tend to eschew "nation building," have designed a military that is better suited to kick down the door, beat up a dictator, and go home than to stay for the harder work of building a democratic polity.

Among a number of possible futures for Iraq are three scenarios that deserve some elaboration. The first is the example of Japan or Germany in 1945, in which the United States stays for seven years and leaves behind a friendly democracy. This would be the preferred outcome, but it is worth remembering that Germany and Japan were ethnically homogeneous societies, ones that also did not produce any terrorist responses to the presence of U.S. troops and could boast significant middle classes that had already experienced democracy in the 1920s. A second scenario is akin to that of Ronald Reagan in Lebanon or Bill Clinton in Somalia, where some of the people who cheered U.S. entry wound up protesting its presence six months later. In this scenario, terrorists kill U.S. soldiers, and the American public reacts by saying, "Saddam is gone, Iraq has no weapons of mass destruction, they don't want our democracy, let's pull out." If this scenario left Iraq in conflict, dictatorship, or theocracy, it would undercut the major post hoc legitimization for the war. The third scenario would be reminiscent of Bosnia or Kosovo. The United States would entice NATO allies and other countries to help in the policing and reconstruction of Iraq, a UN resolution would bless the force, and an international administrator would help to legitimize decisions. The process would be long and frustrating, but it would reduce the prominence of the United States as a target for anti-imperialists and would probably best ensure that America did not pull out prematurely. Ironically, the neo-Wilsonians of the new unilateralist coalition might have to make common cause with the multilateral realists to achieve their objectives. They might find that the world's only superpower can't go it alone after all.

THE PARADOX OF PRIMACY

The Bush administration's new national security strategy correctly identified the challenges growing out of the deep changes in world politics that were illuminated on September 11. But the administration has still not settled on how to implement the new strategy most effectively. Rather than resolving the issue, the second Gulf War leaves the divisions in place, and the real tests still await.

The problem for U.S. power in the twenty-first century is that more and more continues to fall outside the control of even the most powerful state. Although the United States does well on the traditional measures of hard power, these measures fail to capture the ongoing transformation of world politics brought about by globalization and the democratization of technology. The paradox of American power is that world politics is changing in a way that makes it impossible for the strongest world power since Rome to achieve some of its most crucial international goals alone. The United States lacks both the international and the domestic capacity to resolve conflicts that are internal to other societies and to monitor and control transnational developments that threaten Americans at home. On many of today's key issues, such as international financial stability, drug trafficking, the spread of diseases, and especially the new terrorism, military power alone simply cannot produce success, and its use can sometimes be counterproductive. Instead, as the most powerful country, the United States must mobilize international coalitions to address these shared threats and challenges. By devaluing soft power and institutions, the new unilateralist coalition of Jacksonians and neo-Wilsonians is depriving Washington of some of its most important instruments for the implementation of the new national security strategy. If they manage to continue with this tack, the United States could fail what Henry Kissinger called the historical test for this generation of American leaders: to use current preponderant U.S. power to achieve an international consensus behind widely accepted norms that will protect American values in a more uncertain future. Fortunately, this outcome is not preordained.

Terrorism is arguably the most widespread and serious threat to global security today. Not since the Cold War (1945–1990), with its dark prospect of instantaneous nuclear annihilation, have people in the Western world felt less safe in their daily lives. From New York, where terrorists struck on September 11, 2001, to Madrid and London, which suffered later attacks, terrorism poses an ever-present danger to life and limb. Terrorists can bring entire public transportation systems to a grinding halt, interrupt international trade and commerce, and sow confusion on the streets of major cities around the globe. Wherever they go, terrorists carry with them a sinister cargo of fear, disorder, and death.

But where do they come from? More important, what causes them to do what they do? The answer to both questions lies in the long-suspected link between terrorism and failed states, those nations that are incapable of providing for their citizens' basic political and, in some instances, physical needs. Throughout the Middle East and South Asia, failed or failing states routinely prove themselves to be unable to offer anything close to a good life for their people. Poverty, disenfranchisement, frustration, and despair flourish in such conditions, providing the heat that incubates extremist ideologies. In short, many observers contend that corrupt and incompetent governments, and the failing states they run, are the points from which terrorist violence emanates.

Sebastian Mallaby agrees. He argues that the solution to the terrorist problem can be found in the reconstruction of failed states, under the auspices of the American empire. Mallaby, acknowledging American hegemony, would have the United States use its awesome might to fix the political systems of countries whose deficiencies nurture terrorism. This would entail the total removal of dysfunctional regimes according to plans drawn by the United States, working in concert with its allied and client states. Put on the road to success after reconstruction, failed states would no longer contribute to the rise and maintenance of extremist movements. The key, however, is American imperial leadership. As Mallaby writes, "a new imperial moment has arrived, and by virtue of its power, America is bound to play a leading role" in correcting the missteps and misdeeds of failed states.

The Reluctant Imperialist:
Terrorism, Failed States, and the Case for American Empire
SEBASTIAN MALLABY

Lawrence Summers, the dominant professor-politician of the Clinton years, used to say that the United States is history's only nonimperialist superpower. But is this claim anything to boast about today? The war on terrorism has focused attention on the chaotic states that provide profit and sanctuary to nihilist outlaws, from Sudan and Afghanistan to Sierra Leone and Somalia. When such power vacuums threatened great powers in the past, they had a ready solution: imperialism. But since World War II, that option has been ruled out. After more than two millennia of empire, orderly societies now refuse to impose their own institutions on disorderly ones.

This anti-imperialist restraint is becoming harder to sustain, however, as the disorder in poor countries grows more threatening. Civil wars have grown nastier and longer. In a study of 52 conflicts since 1960, a recent World Bank study found that wars started after 1980 lasted three times longer than those beginning in the preceding two decades. Because wars last longer, the number of countries embroiled in them is growing. And the trend toward violent disorder may prove self-sustaining, for war breeds the conditions that make fresh conflict likely. Once a nation descends into violence, its people focus on immediate survival rather than on the longer term. Saving, investment, and wealth creation taper off; government officials seek spoils for their cronies rather than designing policies that might build long-term prosperity. A cycle of poverty, instability, and violence emerges.

There is another reason why state failures may multiply. Violence and social disorder are linked to rapid population growth, and this demographic pressure shows no sign of abating. In the next 20 years, the world's population is projected to grow from around six billion to eight billion, with nearly all of the increase concentrated in poor countries. Some of the sharpest demographic stresses will be concentrated in Afghanistan, Pakistan, Saudi Arabia, Yemen, and the Palestinian territories—all Islamic societies with powerful currents of anti-Western extremism. Only sub-Saharan Africa faces a demographic challenge even sharper than that of the Muslim world. There, an excruciating combination of high birth rates and widespread AIDS infection threatens social disintegration and governmental collapse—which in turn offer opportunities for terrorists to find sanctuary.

Terrorism is only one of the threats that dysfunctional states pose. Much of the world's illegal drug supply comes from such countries, whether opium from Afghanistan or cocaine from Colombia. Other kinds of criminal business flourish under the cover of conflict as well. Sierra Leone's black-market diamonds have benefited a rogues' gallery of thugs, including President Charles Taylor of Liberia and Lebanon's Hezbollah. Failed states also challenge orderly ones by boosting immigration pressures. And those pressures create a lucrative traffic in illegal workers, filling the war chests of criminals.

None of these threats would conjure up an imperialist revival if the West had other ways of responding. But experience has shown that nonimperialist options—notably, foreign aid and various nation-building efforts—are not altogether reliable.

RICH MAN'S BURDEN

Take the chief alternative to imperialism, foreign aid. It is no coincidence that the main multilateral organizations for dispensing it—the United Nations and the World Bank—were set up at the end of World War II as the European empires started to unravel. For decades, the aid intelligentsia was certain that it had the solution to chaos. In the 1950s and 1960s, it thought that simply providing capital would ensure self-sustaining growth in poor countries. In the 1970s, the focus shifted to relieving poverty directly by building health clinics and schools. In the 1980s, donors sought to tie their aid to economic reforms. In the 1990s, they added on demands for anticorruption measures and other improvements in governance. Along the way, development theorists flirted with the idea that population control might hold the key. But no magic key has yet been found. An obstinate group of dysfunctional countries has refused to respond to these approaches.

This is not to say that aid has failed. Since 1960, life expectancy in poor countries has risen from 45 to 64 years. The global illiteracy rate has fallen from 47 to 25 percent over the last three decades. And the number of poor people has fallen by about 200 million in the last two decades—at a time when the world population has increased by 1.6 billion. Development institutions deserve more credit than they get, whether from antiglobalization protesters or from aid critics within Congress and the Bush administration. But aid donors must face up to their inability to shake the most dysfunctional countries out of poverty, especially in regions such as sub-Saharan Africa.

The World Bank has convened an internal task force to confront its record on failed states, and the group will undoubtedly come up with some suggestions. Routing aid around dysfunctional governments is likely to be one of them. But the bank has tried this kind of thing before. In Chad, for example, it spent years devising a plan to develop the country's oil fields while preventing the profits from being wasted by corrupt rulers. An elaborate accounting system was designed in which oil revenues would go into a special fund to pay for health, education, and other worthwhile causes. When the system was unveiled in 2000, the bank even suggested that the "Chadian model" might point the way forward for other resource-rich developing nations. Within six months, however, Chad's government found a way of diverting $4.5 million of oil money to finance unauthorized arms purchases.

In countries such as China and India, which have functioning governments broadly committed to development, aid and technical advice have greatly accelerated the escape from poverty. In Uganda, which has weaker institutions but a fierce dedication to development, aid has helped cut poverty by 40 percent in one decade. But in countries such as Chad, Haiti, or Angola, aid cannot accomplish much. Such places are beyond the reach of economists who prescribe policies from afar. If outsiders want to make a difference in this kind of environment, they must begin by building the institutions that make development possible. They must engage, in other words, in the maligned business of nation building.

NO QUICK FIX

Modern nation building is partly an offshoot of the development business. In the late 1980s, development theorists began to acknowledge that the main alternative to imperialism—economic aid—could not stabilize the weakest states. A political supplement was needed, starting with transparency and other principles of decent governance. This recognition coincided with the collapse of authoritarian regimes—first in Latin America and East Asia, then, more spectacularly, in communist countries. Suddenly dozens of nations found themselves in a state of uncertain transition. The need to focus on the political components of international stability was clear, and a new era of nation building began.

The post–Cold War history of this experiment resembles the history of development aid since World War II. The simple-sounding goal of building stable democracies has proved maddeningly elusive. In turn, nation builders have pushed their strategy through successive stages of elaboration. The sudden collapse of authoritarian regimes first encouraged hopes that democratization might be quick, requiring little more than a simple effort to organize and monitor elections. Later, as transition turned out to be hard, donors sought to build political parties, police forces, law courts, tax offices, central banks, and customs systems—not to mention newspapers, community organizations, and the entire penumbra of independent groups that make up civil society. Within each of these categories, donor efforts have grown more elaborate as well. Rather than simply monitoring elections, for example, nation builders now seek to assess the preceding campaigns to ensure that the playing field is level.

As with development aid, democratization efforts have succeeded in some promising settings. Except for the Balkans, eastern Europe has done well thanks to peace, educated populations, and proximity to the rich European Union. But in the toughest countries, where state failure threatens the export of chaos, nation building has been hard. Perhaps the closest to a success story in a war-torn country is Mozambique, which has remained reasonably stable since foreign peacekeepers pulled out in 1995 after organizing multiparty elections (although that achievement now looks shaky). More typical is Angola, where a 1992 election under U.N. auspices proved worthless because defeated rebels refused to respect the verdict of the polls. In Cambodia, the loser in a 1993 UN-supervised election, Hun Sen's Cambodian People's Party, ignored the results and stayed in power through force. In Bosnia, Kosovo, and East Timor, meanwhile, nation builders are making some headway but are not yet successful enough to withdraw.

To their credit, nation builders have tried to confront this discouraging record. Lakhdar Brahimi, the Algerian diplomat now overseeing the UN's efforts toward Afghanistan, recently produced a report on beefing up the peacekeeping department at the UN's New York headquarters. Out in the field, some peacekeeping operations have been reinforced. The UN went into Sierra Leone with an inadequate contingent of 6,000 in 1999; it now has more than 17,000 troops there. The world has also tried to make up for the UN's peacekeeping inadequacies by sending in other types of forces, with or without a UN umbrella. The West winked at Nigeria's failed effort to impose order on Sierra Leone in 1997, even though Nigeria intervened without a UN mandate. Some observers even argue that mercenaries might carry out more nation-building tasks, as seen in brief deployments in Sierra Leone and Angola.

As with the World Bank's task force on failed states, however, these efforts to beef up nation building are more interesting as implied admissions of failure than as signs of decisive progress. In the absence of greatly increased commitment from the UN's leading member states, a wide gap will remain between nation builders' aspiration to create stable democratic states and what the world's institutions can deliver. Yet the Brahimi report and the occasional calls for a standing UN army recognize the dilemma posed by the end of empire. The rich world increasingly realizes that its interests are threatened by chaos, and that it lacks the tools to fix the problem.

SOMETIMES A GREAT NATION

Might an imperial America arise to fill the gap? Most people would dismiss this as utterly implausible. The United States, it is assumed, has a strong inhibition against external adventurism. Look at the no-passport crowd in Congress, Washington's occasional isolationist fits, and the Bush administration's repeated denunciation of nation building. From the failure to occupy Iraq at the end of the Gulf War to the refusal to commit peacekeeping troops in Afghanistan, the United States has not exactly displayed latent imperialist tendencies.

Yet these inhibitions are less than they appear. U.S. history includes an isolationist tradition, but it is by no means dominant. Other traditions, such as the urge to go forth and improve the world or open up foreign markets, have been present throughout American history as well, and the tradition that prevails at any time is the one that best matches the circumstances. Until the attack on Pearl Harbor in 1941, security seemed assured by brute geography; potential enemies were far across the seas, so foreign policy was often regarded as a luxury. During World War II and the Cold War, that presumption changed. Fascist expansionism and nuclear weapons threatened U.S. interests in obvious ways, and the United States responded with unusual vigor. It fought wars both hot and cold, deploying troops all over the globe. It still spends much more on defense than do the European governments that routinely protest American isolationism.

Now U.S. foreign policy must again respond to circumstance—this time to the growing danger of failed states. The Bush administration's denigration of nation building and its refusal to participate in a peacekeeping force for Afghanistan are not the final words on this subject. By launching his war on terrorism, the president has at least acknowledged the urgency of the threat. For all the grumbling over Balkan commitments, the administration has pulled out of neither Bosnia nor Kosovo. The logic of neoimperialism is too compelling for the Bush administration to resist. The chaos in the world is too threatening to ignore, and existing methods for dealing with that chaos have been tried and found wanting.

MANIFEST DESTINY

Empires are not always planned. The original American colonies began as the unintended byproduct of British religious strife. The British political class was not so sure it wanted to rule India, but commercial interests dragged it in there anyway. The United States today will be an even more reluctant imperialist. But a new imperial moment has arrived, and by virtue of its power America is bound to play the leading role. The question is not whether the United States will seek to fill the void created by the demise of European empires but whether it will acknowledge that this is what it is doing. Only if Washington acknowledges this task will its response be coherent.

The first obstacle to acknowledgment is the fear that empire is infeasible. True, imposing order on failed states is expensive, difficult, and potentially dangerous. Between 1991 and 2000 the United States spent $15 billion on military intervention in the Balkans. A comparable effort in Afghanistan, a much bigger area with deeper traditions of violence, would cost far more. But these expenses need to be set against the cost of fighting wars against terrorists, drug smugglers, and other international criminals. Right after September 11, Congress authorized $40 billion in emergency spending—and that was just a down payment in the struggle against terrorism. The estimated cost to the U.S. economy ranges from $100 billion to $300 billion.

The second obstacle to facing the imperial challenge is the stale choice between unilateralism and multilateralism. Neither option, as currently understood, provides a robust basis for responding to failed states. Unilateralists rightly argue that weak allies and cumbersome multilateral arrangements undercut international engagement. Yet a purely unilateral imperialism is no more likely to work than the sometimes muddled multilateral efforts assembled in the past. Unilateralists need to accept that chaotic countries are more inclined to accept foreign nation builders if they have international legitimacy. And U.S. opinion surveys suggest that international legitimacy matters domestically as well. The American public's support for the Persian Gulf War and the Afghan conflict reflected the perception that each operation was led by the United States but backed by the court of world opinion.

The best hope of grappling with failed states lies in institutionalizing this mix of U.S. leadership and international legitimacy. Fortunately, one does not have to look far to see how this could be accomplished.

The World Bank and the International Monetary Fund (IMF) already embody the same hybrid formula: both institutions reflect American thinking and priorities yet are simultaneously multinational. The mixed record of both institutions—notably the World Bank's failure on failed states—should not obscure their organizational strengths: they are more professional and less driven by national patronage than are UN agencies.

A new international body with the same governing structure could be set up to deal with nation building. It would be subject neither to the frustrations of the U.N. Security Council, with its Chinese and Russian vetoes, nor to those of the U.N. General Assembly, with its gridlocked one-country-one-vote system. A new international reconstruction fund might be financed by the rich countries belonging to the Organization for Economic Cooperation and Development and the other countries that currently contribute to the World Bank's subsidized lending program to the poorest nations. It would assemble nation-building muscle and expertise and could be deployed wherever its American-led board decided, thus replacing the ad hoc begging and arm-twisting characteristic of current peacekeeping efforts. Its creation would not amount to an imperial revival. But it would fill the security void that empires left—much as the system of mandates did after World War I ended the Ottoman Empire.

The new fund would need money, troops, and a new kind of commitment from the rich powers—and it could be established only with strong U.S. leadership. Summoning such leadership is immensely difficult, but America and its allies have no easy options in confronting failed states. They cannot wish away the problem that chaotic power vacuums can pose. They cannot fix it with international institutions as they currently exist. And they cannot sensibly wish for a unilateral American imperium. They must either mold the international machinery to address the problems of their times, as their predecessors did in creating the UN, the World Bank, and the IMF after World War II. Or they can muddle along until some future collection of leaders rises to the challenge.

The terrorist attacks that brought down New York's World Trade Center on September 11, 2001, compelled the United States to flex its imperial muscles. Confronted with a bold challenge offered by a cunning and ruthless opponent, America responded with the naked application of overwhelming military force in Afghanistan. This episode proved to be the prelude to the even larger and more devastating invasion of Iraq. To be sure, in the aftermath of 9/11, American foreign policy became more assertive; some would say excessively so. Indeed, not a few independent observers labeled the United States as an arrogant global bully. Whether or not that was in fact the case, militarily and diplomatically the beginning of the "war on terror" undoubtedly coincided with a more robust American approach to international relations.

This shift has resulted in many changes, not the least of which is an alteration in the American image abroad. A once bright picture of the United States and its intentions has darkened. At one time associated with wealth, political liberty, and cultural freedom, America has become associated with violence, intimidation, and predatory consumerism. America's once iconic status has deteriorated to the point where some people feel more threatened by its overwhelming power than by terrorism. The cumulative effect of such fear and mistrust has been the emergence of an ill-defined and diffuse phenomenon, known simply as "anti-Americanism," that undermines America's effort to build the type of cooperative empire urged by several authors in this volume.

The next essay accepts the basic definition of anti-Americanism as a reaction against America's expanding influence, but contends that it is less a rejection of American hegemony than a response to the absence of balance in world affairs. Anti-Americanism represents, in Ivan Krastev's opinion, a demand for a check on American power and has little to do with America itself. Krastev, in short, argues that anti-Americanism simply fills the void created by the demise of world communism, in particular the erasure of the Soviet Union as a competing superpower. Without a state such as the USSR to balance out American values, ideals, and objectives, America seems to have run amok. Anti-Americanism, then, according to Krastev, is merely the current means through which the rest of the world restrains the American behemoth. Consequently, the United States must address anti-Americanism for what it really is—an expression of unease and a statement of concern about American hegemony. If not viewed as an attempt to reestablish some sensible limits on America's exercise of imperial power, anti-Americanism could provoke a reply from the United States that would garner even more enemies for an already beleaguered empire.

The Anti-American Century?
IVAN KRASTEV

The twentieth century was "the American century." Championing democracy and capitalism, the United States won the Cold War and emerged as the only global superpower—not only in military, but also in economic, technological, and even cultural terms. The widening currency of the English language and the continued desire of millions around the world to emigrate to the United States underlined the reality of U.S. predominance. The future, it was said, looked like a country, and that country was the United States of America.

The terrorist attacks of 11 September 2001, however, sharply punctuated the end of the American century. Indeed, the era we are now entering may well come to be recalled as "the anti-American century." The rise of anti-Americanism around the globe is a distinctive feature of the post–September 11 world. The expressions of anti-Americanism vary from acts of terrorism against American citizens or property to dramatic increases in the global public's negative attitudes toward the United States and its policies, as registered in the latest global polls conducted by the Pew Research Center.[1] Burning American flags, boycotting American commercial products, and mobilizing electoral support through unrestrained anti-American rhetoric are common in many parts of the world. Today there are two basic types of anti-Americanism: murderous anti-Americanism and anti-Americanism "lite." The first is the anti-Americanism of fanatical terrorists who hate the United States, its power, its values, and its policies—and who are willing to kill and to die in order to harm it. The second is the anti-Americanism of those who take to the streets and the media to campaign against America but who do not seek its destruction. The first kind can be dealt with only by "hard power." The second kind, however, must be better understood in order to devise effective strategies to counter it.

It is becoming clear that anti-Americanism is not a passing sentiment and that it cannot be explained simply in terms of the unpopularity of the Bush administration or widespread hostility to the American-led war in Iraq. There is a growing consensus that anti-Americanism is a "master framework" with broad and flexible appeal, and that any serious attempt to analyze the phenomenon must encompass an understanding not only of its various sources in different corners of the world but also of the variety of purposes for which anti-Americanism is used as a political resource.

Some observers rightly argue that anti-Americanism is not a new phenomenon, but they often fail to grasp the importance of its present reemergence. It can be argued that anti-American discourse has not changed much, but what has significantly changed is the world. What matters most is not that America suddenly has become hugely unpopular, but that blaming America has become politically correct behavior even among America' closest allies.

What is new is the way in which anti-Americanism is becoming an instrument in post–Cold War politics. Decoupled from communism, which gave it a certain strength but also placed limits on its appeal, anti-Americanism has worked its way more than ever before into the mainstream of world politics. In a sense, Francis Fukuyama's "end of history" has come to pass, with democracy and capitalism today lacking powerful ideological rivals. But as we arrive at the end of history, we can see anti-Americanism there waiting for us. It has turned into a conjurer's hat, where pieces of different ideologies, anxieties, and political strategies come together to be recombined and recycled for a new life. The appeal of anti-Americanism transcends Left–Right divisions, and it works equally well with anxious governments and angry publics. It fits the definition of an all-purpose ideology. What we are seeing is not so much the rise of anti-Americanism in the singular as the rise of *anti-Americanisms* in the plural. Anti-Americanism assumes different guises in different political contexts. It can even be a prodemocratic force, as it is today in Turkey, though most often it is an antidemocratic rallying point, as in Central and Eastern Europe.

Thus any attempt to find a global explanation for current anti-American sentiments is doomed to fail. The popular view that America is hated for being hostile to Islam may have some explanatory power when applied to the Middle East, but it is a nonstarter in the case of the Balkans, where the United States is hated for being pro-Islamic and pro-Albanian. In Islamic fundamentalist circles, the United States is castigated for being the embodiment of modernity, but Europeans accuse it of not being modern (or postmodern) enough—for practicing capital punishment and for believing too much in God. The United States is blamed both for globalizing the world and for "unilaterally" resisting globalization.

The return of anti-Semitism in Europe and its interconnection with the rise of anti-Americanism also can be interpreted in different ways. One's view of America usually reflects one's view of Israel, and vice-versa. It is easy to believe that many on the European Right are anti-American because America is perceived as pro-Jewish and pro-Israeli. This explanation is more problematic, however, for the European Left, where it seems not that anti-Semites have turned against America but rather that a profound distaste for America has turned Leftists into anti-Zionists and anti-Semites.[2]

AN ELUSIVE DEFINITION

The definition of anti-Americanism will always be elusive. The label cannot and should not be applied to any vocal criticism of U.S. values or policies. Opposition to the policies of the U.S. government surely does not qualify as anti-Americanism. But opposing any policy simply *because* it is endorsed by the U.S. government comes close to being a definition. The trick is to distinguish the sometimes subtle difference between these two stances in real life and in real time. Anti-Americanism is a systemic opposition to America as a whole. It is a critique of the United States that transcends mere disagreement over specific policy questions or government decisions.

The most obvious and logical way to define anti-Americanism would be as opposition to Americanism. The problem is that when you search for "Americanism" on www.google.com or on www.amazon.com, what appears first is James W. Ceaser's article "A Genealogy of Anti-Americanism" and Jean-François Revel's book *Anti-Americanism*. In other words, the current notion of Americanism is to a great extent the invention of anti-American discourse. The fact that any specific political context and any political discourse can invent its own version of America as a hate object gives anti-Americanism its irresistible charm.

The variety of its forms of expression further complicates the study of anti-Americanism: Terrorist acts against American citizens, unfavorable verdicts in opinion polls, commercial boycotts, hostile campaign speeches and media coverage, and graffiti on city walls all appear on the menu of the day. But what are the policy consequences of these very different forms of opposing America? Should the United States be more concerned about countries where anti-American attitudes are prevalent or about countries where the public is basically friendly but the government is overtly anti-American? Terrorists do not require mass anti-American sentiments in order to target American citizens, and there is no certainty that negative perceptions of America registered in opinion polls will have any political consequences.

Historically, dissecting anti-Americanism has been the business of the Right, and this has politically colored all discussion of the subject. In the view of many on the Left, any focus on anti-Americanism is just an excuse to ignore or discredit criticism of U.S. policies. For them, "anti-Americanism" is a protest not against America itself but against its apparent failure to live up to its own ideals. In the words of Chalmers Johnson, "the suicidal assassins of September 11, 2001 did not attack America . . . they attacked American foreign policy."[3] From this perspective, the only meaningful way of analyzing anti-Americanism is to present a critique of U.S. foreign policy.

By contrast, for many Americans on the Right, the rise of anti-Americanism is a rejection of America's civilization and style of life: "They hate our values, not our policies." In this view, a more pro-Arab U.S. policy in the Middle East would not decrease the current levels of anti-Americanism in the Arab world because Arab hatred is driven not by what America does, but by what America is and stands for. Left and Right also take diametrically opposite views regarding the impact of America's military power on the rise of anti-Americanism. In the view of the Left, America is hated for relying too much on its hard power. In the view of the Right, it is America's hesitancy to use its hard power that stimulates the rise of anti-Americanism.[4]

What these two radically different perspectives share is a common conviction that anti-Americanism is about America. But it is precisely this point that is most questionable in my view. For both anti-Americanism and the local responses to it are driven to a significant extent not by concerns about America but by the intrinsic contradictions of postideological politics. Anti-Americanism is becoming a defining political issue in a world that is suffering not from a deficit of elections but from a deficit of politics. Nowadays democracies are societies with invisible enemies and unspoken dreams. Their economies may grow, but people still do not feel happier. In many places in the world, voters feel caught in a trap: They are free to dismiss governments, but they do not feel that they can influence policies. As a result, conspiratorial fantasies have replaced common sense as the basis for public deliberations. This hollowness of postideological and postutopian politics, its subversive dullness, is one of the major reasons for the seductive power of anti-American discourse. People are against America because they are against everything—or because they do not know exactly what they are against.

The latest surveys in Western Europe indicate an important change in the profile of the anti-American constituency. The pattern long typical for France has now become common throughout Western Europe. Elites have become more negative toward the United States than the general public, and younger people are more critical than their elders. Elites in search of legitimacy and a new generation looking for a cause are the two most visible faces of the new European anti-Americanism.

In the aftermath of September 11, America was shocked to discover how hated it is in the Arab world, and Arab anti-Americanism became a special concern of U.S. foreign policy. Yet it is anti-Americanism's resurgence in Western Europe that has made this attitude a major factor in global politics. Hence understanding the split within the EU over U.S. policies toward Iraq is of critical importance for analyzing anti-Americanism's political potential. A reexamination of the controversy over the Iraq war helps to reveal that both the new anti-Americanism in Western Europe and the *anti*-anti-Americanism of the new democracies in Central and Eastern Europe have almost nothing to do with Iraq and very little to do with America.

EUROPE AND THE ANTI-AMERICAN TEMPTATION

Politics often demands the manufacturing of useful clichés. So when British prime minister Tony Blair, in his July 2003 speech before a joint session of the U.S. Congress, stated that the EU's new members will transform Europe "because their scars are recent, their memories strong, their relationship with freedom still one of passion, not comfortable familiarity," he was practicing good politics. But good politics does not always make for sound explanations. Some American conservatives were even more persistent than Blair in stressing the "value dimension" in the decision of East European governments to ally with the United States regarding Iraq. The only problem with this analysis is that it is not supported by the polls. Public opinion surveys indicated that there was a strong antiwar majority (70 to 75 percent) in all the postcommunist countries. The "coalition of the willing" was really a "coalition of the reluctant." The only difference between Sofia and Berlin was that in Sofia the antiwar majority was visible only in the polls, not on the streets. The conservatives' reading of events was equally wrong with respect to the motivations of East European elites. The "commitment to freedom" argument may explain the support that the United States received from former dissidents such as Václav Havel and Adam Michnik, but it can hardly account for the behavior of the ex-communist governments that today run half of New Europe. "Commitment to freedom" was never their trademark.

Washington's opponents were quick to label New Europe's falling into line as "the march of the vassals." In their view, the conspicuous loyalty that these governments demonstrated toward the United States was not much different from the loyalty that they used to display toward the Soviet Union in the days of the Cold War. Far from a commitment to freedom, it was the instinct of the vassal whose behavior is motivated by carrots and sticks that explains the course taken by East European governments. This interpretation is also difficult to justify. In terms of power politics, France and Germany, with the European Commission behind them, were able both to wield bigger sticks and to offer bigger carrots to the East European countries than was the United States. So if the satellite mentality had really been at work, New Europe should have gone "Old."

In short, neither a commitment to freedom nor the satellite mentality offers an adequate explanation for East European support for Washington. The real difference between Poland and France was their differing judgments about the advantages and risks attendant upon encouraging anti-American sentiments. Paris looked at the rise of anti-Americanism and saw an opportunity for increasing French influence in the world. Warsaw looked at the same phenomenon and saw a threat to all its hard-won gains from a decade of arduous political and economic reforms.

THE ANTI-ANTI-AMERICANISM OF NEW EUROPE

The real cause of the division between Old and New Europe during the Iraq war was the seductive charm of anti-American rhetoric for certain West European leaders. For New Europe, by contrast, flirting with anti-Americanism was not simply in bad taste, it was politically dangerous. Postcommunist governments have important domestic political reasons for worrying about the rise of anti-Americanism. The democratic and market changes that Eastern Europe experienced over the past decade came wrapped in the American flag. When democracy came to Eastern Europe, it was singing in English, it was in love with the U.S. Constitution, and it was promoted by American foundations. For the reformist elites in postcommunist countries, attacks on America appeared politically (and not just symbolically) subversive.

Another major factor dividing Europeans was the conflicting legacies of 1968. In Western Europe, the protestors of 1968 were openly anti-American and in many respects anticapitalist. In their view, the United States was "Amerika"—the very embodiment of imperialism and capitalist exploitation. In the imagination of the 1968 generation in the East, however, America was the symbol of democracy and the free world. When German student leader Rudi Dutschke went on a solidarity tour in 1968 to Prague to ask Czech students to join in a common struggle against capitalist democracy and the dictatorship of the market, Czech students told him that this was exactly what they were struggling *for*. For Western Europe, "the third way" was a road to escape from capitalism; for Poles and Czechs, it was a road to escape from socialism. This difference in the socialization of many of the political and cultural elites now in power in Europe led to their divergent reactions to the rise of anti-Americanism during the Iraq crisis. Both Berlin and Warsaw remained loyal to the legacy of 1968, but it is a legacy that divides East and West.

East Europeans were quick to realize that the recent wave of anti-Americanism, celebrated by some of their Western neighbors as marking the birth of a genuine European public, posed a clear and present danger of delegitimizing the East's reformist elites and reversing their policies. At a time when many people in postcommunist Europe have been feeling let down by the "decade of change," anti-American rhetoric, once declared legitimate in Paris or Berlin, opens the door to populist parties of both Left and Right. In the words of Ian Buruma, "European populism historically almost always was anti-American."[5]

A June 2003 public opinion survey conducted by the Centre for Liberal Strategies and BBSS Gallup International in five Balkan countries underlines the validity of Buruma's point.[6] In responses to this survey, hostility to the United States correlates with hostility to markets and democracy, as well as hostility toward Jews. Those parts of the public that are favorable to the United States are also the most prodemocratic and the most favorable toward the EU. In the Balkans, in contrast to Western Europe, it is the younger, better-educated, and more active part of the population that most often expresses positive attitudes toward the United States. Thus New Europe's political elites perceive the U.S.–EU rivalry as an extremely negative factor in their efforts to reform their own societies. In the early 1990s, Eastern Europe was ready to embrace democracy in large part because democracy was associated with the American dream. Today many East European politicians and intellectuals side with America because they understand that in the local context the fashion for blaming America is opening the door to attacks on democracy and the market.

Antidemocratic forces in the East, lacking any positive vision for an alternative future and inspired by growing public criticism of the status quo, see anti-Americanism as a catchall platform for protest-vote politics. The power of anti-Americanism lies in its very emptiness. For politicians such as Serbia's Vojislav Seselj (who is currently awaiting trial before a UN war-crimes tribunal at the Hague), anti-Americanism provides an opportunity to recast the nationalist agenda at a moment when Serbs are no longer ready to die for Kosovo or to kill for Bosnia. For the old communist elites in countries like Bulgaria, the new political correctness of anti-Americanism offers a way to reinsert themselves into the democratic political landscape on their own terms. It is astonishing to observe how many ex-communists in Eastern Europe embrace the notion of Europe as the anti-America. For this new New Old Left, blaming America is a strategy for pitting democracy against capitalism.

For some corrupt postcommunist governments, anti-Americanism is an instrument for redirecting public anger. For disillusioned publics, anti-Americanism is a vehicle for expressing anger at their betrayal by the elites. Although socialist solutions are considered dead in these "end of history" societies, socialist *attitudes* are as alive as ever. When winning the protest vote is the name of the game, anti-Americanism is the favorite tactic.

The anti-anti-Americanism of New Europe is usually perceived as simple pro-Americanism, but the failure to appreciate the distinction between these two concepts can have grave consequences. Some political circles in Washington flirt with the idea of using New Europe as an instrument for dividing and weakening the EU with respect to foreign and security policy. Such a strategy would be based on dangerously unrealistic assumptions. The decision of almost all the new democracies to side with the EU over the International Criminal Court should be a sign to American policy makers that taking Eastern Europe's support for granted would be a major foreign policy miscalculation. For East Europeans, backing the United States during the Iraq crisis was a triumph of history over geography. But history itself teaches us that geography is stronger in the long run.

Nonetheless, New Europe has strong political (and not merely sentimental) reasons to resist the tendency to make anti-Americanism the foundation of a united Europe. For neo-Gaullists and die-hard social democrats, Europe is the center of a new world that will confront America in the same way that the old New World had confronted monarchical Europe in the eighteenth century. In their view, anti-Americanism should be the common European political language. Europe's new democracies do not share this view.

The problem with the European challenge to America is that Europe sees this competition less as an opportunity for promoting its existing model of welfare capitalism and more as a tactic to buy public support for profoundly transforming this model in a more market-oriented direction. The reality is that the EU is becoming less and less "European" in terms of pursuing the welfare-state policies developed in postwar Western Europe. It is striking to observe that when the EU supports projects to promote economic development beyond its borders, it exports a version of the same type of neoliberal orthodoxy that it denounces at home. New Europe's rejection of the negative definition of European identity supplied by anti-Americanism is its real contribution to the European debate. United Europe needs a positive identity.

At present Europe and America are allies divided by common values and common interests.

THE DANGEROUS CHARM OF ANTI-AMERICANISM

There are strange functional similarities among the three discourses that largely shape global politics today—antiterrorism, anticorruption, and anti-Americanism. All three of them flourish at the end of history, when no universal alternative to democracy and the market is in play, but disappointment with democracy and the market is growing. Today democracy may often be redefined or distorted but it is not openly opposed. Antimarket and anticapitalist sentiments are enjoying a subterranean resurgence, but on the surface they take the form of a debate between Joseph Stiglitz and the International Monetary Fund (IMF). What used to be a class struggle has now been reduced to a quarrel in the faculty lounge. The three dominant discourses are "empty boxes," easily filled with vague anxieties and cynically designed political strategies; each is a response to the growing gap between voting publics and their democratically elected elites. All three discourses can be used to criticize the status quo without incurring the odium of openly attacking democracy or the market. Groups with totally conflicting purposes can exploit all three to serve their own agendas.

When anticorruption rhetoric burst upon the stage of global politics in the early 1990s, it was conceptualized as a way to mobilize support for deepening market and democratic reforms. Anticorruption campaigns were designed as a coordinated effort by civil society and the international community (the World Bank, the IMF, and Western governments) to pressure national governments into delivering good governance. The anticorruption rhetoric shared by Washington and local civil society actors was intended to answer the question of what had gone wrong. Mass publics were ready to sign on. But the result has been that political competition in many democracies is now reduced to a confrontation between a government accused of corruption and an opposition that claims to be slightly less corrupt. Anticorruption campaigns have undermined politics understood as a matter of representative government and clashing ideas and programs. Far from contributing to a narrowing of the gap between publics and elites, anticorruption discourse has enlarged the gap.

When terrorism captured the global imagination after 9/11, antiterrorist discourse was designed to highlight the common threat that would help shore up the new world order. In fact, however, various governments have hijacked the antiterrorist agenda in order to destroy their local political opposition and to gain control over civil society. Antiterrorist discourse has been skillfully used to foster suspicion of NGOs and independent media and to curb civil liberties.

Governments seized the opportunity and started manufacturing terrorists. A successful mixture of antiterrorist and anticorruption rhetoric, moderate anti-Americanism, and old-style administrative politics has enabled Vladimir Putin to consolidate an "acceptable" authoritarian regime in Russia. This model has the potential to be replicated. Governments that had found their freedom of action modestly weakened by the spread of democracy and global interdependence have used antiterrorism to bolster their control and enhance the secrecy of their operations.

The impact of anti-American discourse is likely to be similarly harmful to democracy. Washington adopted a high profile in promoting the anticorruption agenda, attempting to bypass governments by telling civil society actors that corrupt governments are the problem. In the case of antiterrorism, Washington allowed discredited governments to label their domestic opponents as terrorists in return for support in the global "war on terrorism." In the case of anti-Americanism, governments are trying to convince frustrated publics that America is the problem. The anticorruption drive was designed to promote the spread of capitalism and deepen democracy. It failed. Antiterrorist discourse was designed to rally the world around America. It failed. Anti-Americanism has emerged as a hostile response to America's growing influence but also to the spread of democracy and the global market. Unfortunately, it has a chance to succeed.

AMERICAN RESPONSES TO ANTI-AMERICANISM

In the immediate aftermath of September 11, the United States viewed public diplomacy as the proper response to the rise of anti-Americanism. A Council on Foreign Relations report declared that improving the U.S. image through public diplomacy is directly linked to the country's most fundamental national security needs.[7] Now the strategy has changed. Aggressive democracy promotion is America's current response to both terrorism and anti-Americanism. Can it work?

It is true that the United States has been most popular and powerful when it allied itself with the cause of democracy and freedom. This is the lesson that America learns from its own history. But democracy promotion can suffer collateral damage from the unholy struggle among the discourses of anticorruption, antiterrorism, and anti-Americanism that shape our world today. The threat of terrorism has already confronted democratic societies with the need to renegotiate the borders between civil liberties and public safety. Each society should answer on its own the question of how much freedom it is ready to sacrifice to have a better chance to defend itself in the face of the global terrorist threat. The problem is when the answers are given not by society but by undemocratic governments.

The new security focus in American foreign policy has resulted in its inflating the democratic credentials of a number of tyrannies, beginning with those in Central Asia. The way in which the U.S. government handles the tradeoff between democratic performance and security cooperation can antagonize democratic movements in some places and become a real obstacle to promoting the democratic agenda. Washington paid the price for such policies in Latin America in the days of the Cold War, and it is paying the price for such policies in the Middle East today. Yet ignoring the reality of the terrorist threat is not an option. The objective of combating terrorism through military and police cooperation and the objective of spreading democracy will remain in tension and at times even in outright conflict.

The rise of anti-Americanism could become a major obstacle to promoting democracy in the world. In the context of the new suspicion of the United States and its policies, many nondemocratic, semi-democratic, or even almost-democratic regimes are tempted to criminalize any internal pressure for democracy, labeling it "American-sponsored destabilization." The recent events in Georgia provide a classic illustration of this point. At the very moment when Georgians took to the streets in defense of their right to fair elections, then-president Eduard Shevardnadze was quick to label the popular movement an American-inspired conspiracy. The strategy of authoritarian governments is to try to force democratic movements to dissociate themselves from the United States, thus isolating them and depriving them of international support. For the United States, democracy promotion is a vehicle for winning the hearts and minds of people around the world. But if anti-Americanism can succeed in identifying pressure for democracy with "American imperialism," this will undermine the prospects for the spread of democracy.

The transatlantic rift increases this risk. Guided by the under-standable desire to protect themselves from the rising wave of anti-Americanism, many European governments and foundations are trying to distance themselves from American democracy-promotion efforts in environments where there is strong antipathy to the United States. This stance can jeopardize any chance for democratic break-throughs in many parts of the world. The democratic momentum of the 1990s was possible because Europe and America shared a common democratization agenda; in many areas, their democracy-promotion programs were coordinated. A trans-Atlantic divide in the field of democracy promotion will erode the very idea of internationally backed democratization efforts.

America's new commitment to spreading democracy will face another critical challenge. The miracle of 1989 cannot be repeated. In Eastern Europe, democratization gave birth to pro-American governments and pro-American societies. A similar result cannot be expected in the Middle East or some other parts of the world. Iraq is not another Poland. Faced with the prospect of the emergence of anti-American democracies that present a security risk for the United States, Washington may be forced to trim its democratization agenda. But such a reaction could have a grave impact on the politics of democratization as a whole. It might result in the adoption of democracy-building strategies that are "security-sensitive," and where democracy is misconceived as a political regime that can redirect and keep under control local conflicts, even if it fails to provide much freedom. Introducing free elections into ethnically divided societies is not equivalent to democratizing these societies. Weak and nonfunctioning states are as much a threat to freedom and human rights as the oppressive governments that they have replaced. The Middle East will provide the stiffest test of whether U.S. democratization strategies can remain committed to the principle that democracy also means an open society.

What America has failed to recognize until now is that in many places in the world the rise of anti-Americanism provokes the emergence of anti-anti-American constituencies. Even when they disagree with U.S. policies, these constituencies understand that less American influence means less freedom, and that anti-Americanism is a stalking horse and platform for antidemocratic and antimarket forces. This naturally emerging, homegrown anti-anti-Americanism offers the United States its best means for countering the politics of anti-Americanism. In other words, it is *supporting* democracy, more than *exporting* it, that constitutes America's best strategic option.

NOTES

The author is deeply grateful to the German Marshall Fund of the United States for supporting the work of the Centre for Liberal Strategies on anti-Americanism.

1. See "Views of a Changing World 2003: War With Iraq Further Divides Global Publics," http://people-press.org/reports/display.php3?ReportID=185.

2. Historically the Left has denounced the instrumentalization of anti-Semitism in European politics.

3. Chalmers Johnson, *Blowback: The Costs and Consequences of American Empire*, 2nd ed. New York: Henry Holt, 2002, viii.

4. As Barry Rubin has written, "It has been the United States's perceived softness in recent years, rather than its bullying behavior, that has encouraged the anti-Americans to act on their beliefs." Barry Rubin, "The Real Roots of Arab Anti-Americanism," *Foreign Affairs* 81 (November–December 2002): 83.

5. *Financial Times* (London), 9 January 2004.

6. The "Anti-Americanism in the Balkans" survey was conducted by BBSS Gallup International and funded by the Open Society Foundation in Sofia. The survey covers Bulgaria, Macedonia, Kosovo, Romania, and Serbia.

7. To view the Council on Foreign Relations report, see www.cfr.org/pubs/Task-force_final2-19.pdf.

Bibliography

———— ⚭ ————

Boot, Max. "Neither New nor Nefarious: The Liberal Empire Strikes Back." *Current History*, 102 (November 2003) 667: 361–366.

Cumings, Bruce. "Is America an Imperial Power?" *Current History*, 102 (November 2003) 667: 355–260.

Haass, Richard N. "What to Do With American Primacy." *Foreign Affairs*, 78 (September/October 1999) 5: 37–49.

Ikenberry, G. John. "American and the Ambivalence of Power." *Current History*, 102 (November 2003) 667: 377–382.

Jervis, Robert. "The Compulsive Empire." *Foreign Policy* (July/August 2003). Online at www.foreignpolicy.com/story/cms.php?story_id=93&print=1, 7/2/2005.

Judis, John B. "Imperial Amnesia." *Foreign Policy* (July/August 2004). Online at www.foreignpolicy.com/story/cms.php?story_id=2582&print=1, 7/2/2005.

Khanna, Parag. "The Counsel of Geploitics." *Current History*, 102 (November 2003) 667: 388–393.

Klare, Michael T. "The Empire's New Frontiers." *Current History*, 102 (November 2003) 667: 383–387.

Krastev, Ivan. "The Anti-American Century." *Journal of Democracy*, 15 (April 2004) 2: 5–16.

Mallaby, Sebastian. "The Reluctant Imperialist: Terrorism, Failed States, and the Case for American Empire." *Foreign Affairs*, 81 (March/April 2003) 2: 2–7.

Nye, Joseph S. Jr. "U.S. Power and Strategy After Iraq." *Foreign Affairs*, 82 (July/August 2003) 4: 60–73.

Simes, Dimitri K. "America's Imperial Dilemma." *Foreign Affairs*, 82 (November/December 2003) 6: 91–102.

Sources Cited

Egnal, Marc. *A Mighty Empire: The Origins of the American Revolution.* Ithaca: Cornell University Press, 1988.

Davis, Zev. "The Ottomanization of the United States," Middle East Times, 29 March 2005. Online at www.metimes.com/print. php?StoryID=20050329-061238-4548r, 7/3/2005.

Ferguson, Niall. *Empire: The Rise and Demise of the British World Order and the Lessons for Global Power.* New York: Basic Books, 2004.

Karp, Walter. *The Politics of War: The Story of Two Wars Which Altered Forever the Political Life of the American Republic.* New York: Harper Colophon Books, 1979.

Kennedy, Paul. *The Rise and Fall of the Great Powers: Economic Change and Military Conflict from 1500–2000.* New York: Random House, 1987.

Meyer, Karl. *The Dust of Empire: The Race for Mastery in the Asian Heartland.* New York: Public Affairs, 2003.

Roberts, J.A.G. *A Concise History of China.* Cambridge, Massachusetts: Harvard University Press, 1999.

Santosuosso, Antonio. *Storming the Heavens: Soldiers, Emperors, and Civilians in the Roman Empire.* Boulder, Colorado: Westview Press, 2001.

Tucker, Robert W. and David C. Hendrickson. *Empire of Liberty: The Statecraft of Thomas Jefferson.* New York: Oxford University Press, 1990.

Further Reading

———◦≫◦———

Books

Barber, Benjamin R. *Fear's Empire: War, Terrorism, and Democracy.* New York: W.W. Norton and Company, 2003.

Boot, Max. *The Savage Wars of Peace: Small Wars and the Rise of American Power.* New York: Basic Books, 2003.

Ferguson, Niall. *Colossus: The Price of America's Empire.* New York: Penguin Press, 2004.

Johnson, Chalmers. *The Sorrows of Empire: Militarism, Secrecy, and the End of the Republic.* New York: Metropolitan Books, 2004.

Kaplan, Robert D. *Imperial Grunts: The American Military on the Ground.* New York: Random House, 2005.

Merry, Robert W. *Sands of Empire: Missionary Zeal, American Foreign Policy, and the Hazards of Global Ambition.* New York: Simon and Schuster, 2005.

Munn Michael. *Incoherent Empire.* New York: Verso, 2003.

Todd, Emmanuel. *After the Empire: The Breakdown of the American Order.* New York: Columbia University Press, 2003.

Web Sites

Maier, Charles S. "An American Empire?" Harvard Magazine. Available online at www.harvardmagazine.com/on-line/1102193.html.

The American Empire Project. Available online at www.american empireproject.com.

Todd, Emmanuel. "The Conceited Empire." The Dominion. Available online at http://dominionpaper.ca/features/2003/the_conceited_ empire.html.

Index

About the Editor

———∞∞∞———

JOHN C. DAVENPORT holds a Ph.D. from the University of Connecticut and currently teaches at Corte Madera School in Portola Valley, California. Davenport is the author of several biographies, including one about Muslim leader Saladin, and has written extensively on the role of borders in American history. He lives in San Carlos, California, with his wife, Jennifer, and his two sons, William and Andrew.